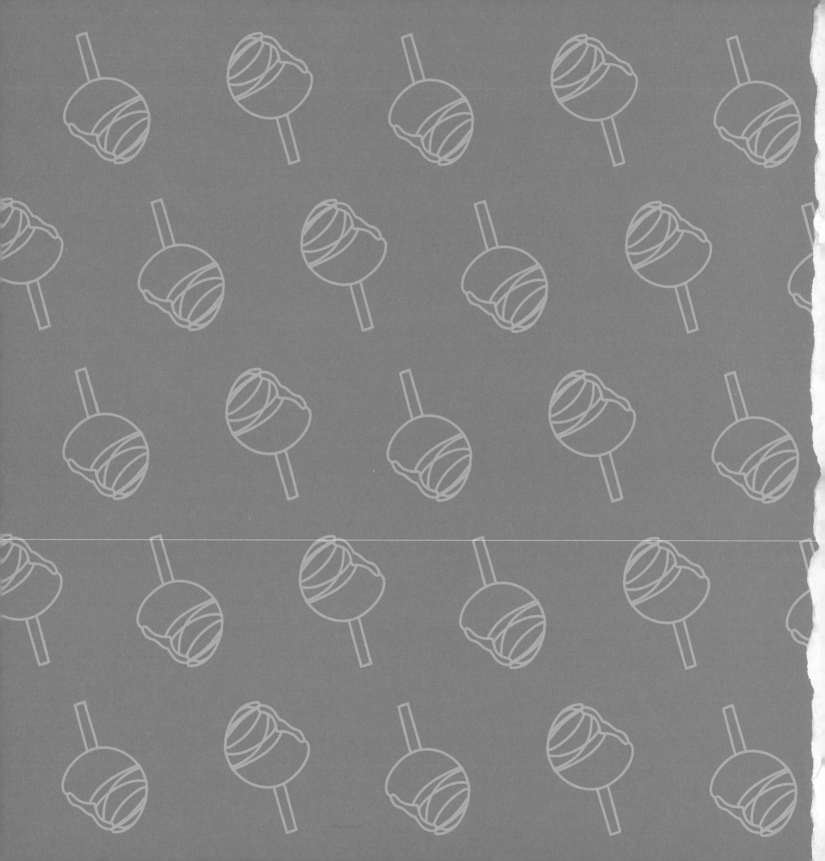

Fun Stuff

Cake Pops

& Mini Treats

Publications International, Ltd.

Pictured on the front cover *(clockwise from top left):* Little Ladybugs *(page 16)*, Nice Mice *(page 8)*, Banana Split Ice Cream Sandwiches *(page 88)* and Pink Pig Pops *(page 10)*.
Pictured on the jacket flaps: Funky Monkeys *(page 14)* and Tiny Peanut Butter Sandwiches *(page 82)*.
Pictured on the back cover *(left to right):* Tweet Treats *(page 12)*, Fun Frogs *(page 6)* and Pumpkin Whoopie Minis *(page 84)*.

ISBN-13: 978-1-4508-3727-9
ISBN-10: 1-4508-3727-1

Library of Congress Control Number: 2011935086

Manufactured in China.

8 7 6 5 4 3 2 1

Microwave Cooking: Microwave ovens vary in wattage. Use the cooking times as guidelines and check for doneness before adding more time.

Preparation/Cooking Times: Preparation times are based on the approximate amount of time required to assemble the recipe before cooking, baking, chilling or serving. These times include preparation steps such as measuring, chopping and mixing. The fact that some preparations and cooking can be done simultaneously is taken into account. Preparation of optional ingredients and serving suggestions is not included.

Publications International, Ltd.

Contents

So What's a Cake Pop?

Cake pops are bite-size treats made of crumbled cake mixed with frosting and covered in candy coating. They're very easy to make—especially when you use cake mixes and prepared frosting—and decorating them can be as simple or as challenging as you want. Just read through the tips below to help you get started.

Ingredients for Sweet Success

• You can use any kind of cake to make cake pops—use your favorite 13×9-inch cake recipe instead of a mix if you prefer. You may want to bake the cake a day ahead of time since it needs to be completely cool before crumbling.

• The frosting, like the cake, can be homemade or store-bought. Homemade buttercream and cream cheese frostings work well, and if you make your own frosting, you can use less sugar to balance the sweetness in the cake and the candy coating. But canned frostings (any variety except whipped) are a convenient option with many different flavors to choose from.

• Candy coating can be found in a wide variety of colors and flavors at craft and specialty stores. (You might have already seen it in its basic chocolate and vanilla or almond versions in the supermarket, where it's called bark or confectionary coating.) Candy coating should be stored in a cool, dry place at room temperature, never refrigerated or frozen.

1-2-3 Pop!

1. The first step in making cake pops is crumbling the cake. It's easy to crumble cake with your hands, but you can also use a food processor to do the job. You should end up with fine crumbs and no large cake pieces remaining.

2. Next, mix in the frosting. Again, it's easiest to do this with your hands, but a spoon or spatula works well if you don't want to get your hands messy. The mixture should be moist enough to roll into balls, but not so wet or heavy that the balls won't hold their shape.

3. Finally, roll the mixture into balls or other shapes with your hands and put them on a waxed paper-lined baking sheet. Cover and refrigerate for a few hours until they're firm.

Dipping & Decorating

• To transform a ball of cake and frosting into irresistible edible art, you need plenty of candy coating. Place the coating in a deep microwavable container (drinking glasses work well) and microwave on MEDIUM (50%) for 1 minute. Stir, then microwave for additional 30-second intervals until the coating is completely melted, stirring after each interval. Be careful not to overheat the coating. It's best to use the coating as is, especially when you're first getting started, but if you find the coating to be too thick, you can thin it slightly by adding a small amount of vegetable oil or shortening. Heating the coating longer won't make it any thinner.

• For each cake pop, dip a lollipop stick about ½ inch into the melted candy coating, then insert the stick into the cake ball (no more than halfway through). After a few minutes to set, the cake pops can be dipped.

• Before you start dipping, make sure you have your decorations and a foam block nearby. (Floral foam blocks work particularly well.) If you'll be adding decorations you want to adhere while the coating is wet (for example, the ears on the Funky Monkeys, page 14), you have a short window of time (about a minute) to arrange these candies on the pops before the coating sets. But if you aren't able to attach the decorations at this point, don't worry. The melted coating acts as a very strong glue, and you can simply use a toothpick to place dots of coating on the pop wherever you want to attach your candies. Hold them in place until the coating sets.

Cake Pop Pointers

• For recipes with lighter coatings, it's best to choose lighter cakes and frostings so the cake doesn't show through.

• If you put your cake pops in the freezer rather than the refrigerator to firm them up quickly, make sure they don't freeze solid (or if they do, let them warm up a little before dipping). The warm melted coating doesn't work as well on frozen surfaces.

• If you don't find the color of candy coating you want, you can combine different color coatings to create a new shade. You can also tint the coating with candy coloring, but be sure to use oil-based candy coloring and not regular food coloring.

• Arranging small sprinkles and decors on a little cake pop can be frustrating. Try using tweezers to place the decorations exactly where you want them—you can find inexpensive tweezers at craft stores.

Critter Pops

Fun Frogs

½ baked and cooled 13×9-inch cake
½ cup plus 2 tablespoons frosting
1 package (14 to 16 ounces) green candy coating
24 lollipop sticks
   Foam block
   White fruit-flavored pastel candy wafers
   Chocolate sprinkles
   Black string licorice, cut into 1¼-inch lengths
   Black decorator frosting

1. Line large baking sheet with waxed paper. Use hands to crumble cake into large bowl. Add frosting to cake crumbs; mix with hands until well blended. Shape mixture into 1½-inch balls (about 2 tablespoons cake mixture per ball); place on prepared baking sheet. Cover with plastic wrap; refrigerate at least 1 hour or freeze 10 minutes to firm.

2. When cake balls are firm, place candy coating in deep microwavable bowl. Melt according to package directions. Dip one lollipop stick about ½ inch into melted coating; insert stick into cake ball (no more than halfway through). Return cake pop to baking sheet in refrigerator to set. Repeat with remaining cake balls and sticks.

3. Working with one cake pop at a time, hold stick and dip cake ball into melted coating to cover completely, letting excess coating drip off. Rotate stick gently and/or tap stick on edge of bowl, if necessary, to remove excess coating. Place cake pop in foam block. Immediately attach two candy wafers to top of pop for eyes while coating is still wet; hold in place until coating is set.

4. Dip toothpick in candy coating; place two dots of coating on cake pops to attach sprinkles for nose. Apply coating to one side of each licorice piece; press onto cake pops for smile. Pipe dot of black frosting in each eye.

Makes about 24 pops

Nice Mice

½ baked and cooled 13×9-inch cake*
½ cup plus 2 tablespoons frosting
1 package (14 to 16 ounces) chocolate candy coating
24 lollipop sticks
Foam block
Additional chocolate candy coating discs**
White round candies
Small pink candies, mini candy-coated chocolate pieces or decors
Black decorator frosting

*Prepare a cake from a mix according to package directions or use your favorite recipe. Cake must be cooled completely.
**Large chocolate nonpareil candies can also be used.

1. Line large baking sheet with waxed paper. Use hands to crumble cake into large bowl. (You should end up with fine crumbs and no large cake pieces remaining.)

2. Add frosting to cake crumbs; mix with hands until well blended. Shape mixture into 1½-inch balls (about 2 tablespoons cake mixture per ball); place on prepared baking sheet. Cover with plastic wrap; refrigerate at least 1 hour or freeze 10 minutes to firm.

3. When cake balls are firm, place candy coating in deep microwavable bowl. Melt according to package directions. Dip one lollipop stick about ½ inch into melted coating; insert stick into cake ball (no more than halfway through). Return cake pop to baking sheet in refrigerator to set. Repeat with remaining cake balls and sticks.

4. Working with one cake pop at a time, hold stick and dip cake ball into melted coating to cover completely, letting excess coating drip off. Rotate stick gently and/or tap stick on edge of bowl, if necessary, to remove excess coating. Place cake pop in foam block. Immediately attach two chocolate discs to top of pop for ears while coating is still wet; hold in place until coating is set.

5. Dip toothpick in candy coating; place two dots of coating on cake pops to attach white candies for eyes. Add dot of coating and pink candy for nose. Pipe dot of black frosting in each eye.   *Makes about 24 pops*

Tip: To add tails, roll small pieces of chewy chocolate candies between your hands into very thin ropes. Attach to mice using melted candy coating.

Nice Mice

Pink Pig Pops

½ baked and cooled 13×9-inch cake*
½ cup plus 2 tablespoons frosting
  Pink chewy fruit candy squares or taffy strips
1 package (14 to 16 ounces) pink candy coating
24 lollipop sticks
  Foam block
  Mini semisweet chocolate chips
  Pink fruit-flavored pastel candy wafers
  Black decorator frosting

Prepare a cake from a mix according to package directions or use your favorite recipe. Cake must be cooled completely.

1. Line large baking sheet with waxed paper. Use hands to crumble cake into large bowl. (You should end up with fine crumbs and no large cake pieces remaining.)

2. Add frosting to cake crumbs; mix with hands until well blended. Shape mixture into 1½-inch balls (about 2 tablespoons cake mixture per ball); place on prepared baking sheet. Cover with plastic wrap; refrigerate at least 1 hour or freeze 10 minutes to firm.

3. Meanwhile, prepare ears. Working with one at a time, unwrap candy squares and microwave on LOW (30%) 5 seconds or until softened. Press candies between hands or on waxed paper to flatten to ⅛-inch thickness. Use scissors or paring knife to cut out triangles for ears. Bend tips of ears, if desired.

4. When cake balls are firm, place candy coating in deep microwavable bowl. Melt according to package directions. Dip one lollipop stick about ½ inch into melted coating; insert stick into cake ball (no more than halfway through). Return cake pop to baking sheet in refrigerator to set. Repeat with remaining cake balls and sticks.

5. Working with one cake pop at a time, hold stick and dip cake ball into melted coating to cover completely, letting excess coating drip off. Rotate stick gently and/or tap stick on edge of bowl, if necessary, to remove excess coating. Place cake pop in foam block. Immediately attach two candy ears to top of pop while coating is still wet; hold in place until coating is set.

6. Dip toothpick in candy coating; place two dots of coating on cake pops to attach mini chips for eyes. (Cut off pointed tips of chips so chips will lay flat.) Add dot of coating and candy wafer for nose. Pipe two dots of black frosting on each nose. *Makes about 24 pops*

Tip: To add tails, roll small pieces of softened candy squares between your hands into thin ropes. Curl tails; attach to pigs using melted candy coating.

Pink Pig Pops

Tweet Treats

½ baked and cooled 13×9-inch cake*
½ cup plus 2 tablespoons frosting
    Yellow and orange chewy fruit candy squares or taffy strips
1 package (14 to 16 ounces) yellow candy coating
24 lollipop sticks
    Foam block
    Black decorator frosting

Prepare a cake from a mix according to package directions or use your favorite recipe. Cake must be cooled completely.

1. Line large baking sheet with waxed paper. Use hands to crumble cake into large bowl. (You should end up with fine crumbs and no large cake pieces remaining.)

2. Add frosting to cake crumbs; mix with hands until well blended. Shape mixture into 1½-inch balls (about 2 tablespoons cake mixture per ball); place on prepared baking sheet. Cover with plastic wrap; refrigerate at least 1 hour or freeze 10 minutes to firm.

3. Meanwhile, prepare decorations. Working with one at a time, unwrap yellow candy squares and microwave on LOW (30%) 5 seconds or until softened. Press candies between hands or on waxed paper to flatten to ⅛-inch thickness. Use scissors or paring knife to cut out triangles for wings and top feathers. Repeat procedure with orange candy squares, pressing candies thinner (1/16 inch) and cutting into smaller triangles for beaks.

4. When cake balls are firm, place candy coating in deep microwavable bowl. Melt according to package directions. Dip one lollipop stick about ½ inch into melted coating; insert stick into cake ball (no more than halfway through). Return cake pop to baking sheet in refrigerator to set. Repeat with remaining cake balls and sticks.

5. Working with one cake pop at a time, hold stick and dip cake ball into melted coating to cover completely, letting excess coating drip off. Rotate stick gently and/or tap stick on edge of bowl, if necessary, to remove excess coating. Place cake pop in foam block. Immediately attach two yellow triangles to sides of pop for wings while coating is still wet; hold in place until coating is set.

6. Dip toothpick in candy coating; place dots of coating on cake pops to attach top feathers. Add dots of coating and two orange triangles for beak. Pipe two dots of black frosting above beak for eyes.

Makes about 24 pops

Tweet Treats

Funky Monkeys

½ baked and cooled 13×9-inch cake*
½ cup plus 2 tablespoons frosting
   Small chewy chocolate candies
 1 package (14 to 16 ounces) chocolate candy coating
24 lollipop sticks
   Foam block
   Brown candy-coated chocolate pieces
   Round yellow candies
   Black and yellow decorator frosting

Prepare a cake from a mix according to package directions or use your favorite recipe. Cake must be cooled completely.

1. Line large baking sheet with waxed paper. Use hands to crumble cake into large bowl. (You should end up with fine crumbs and no large cake pieces remaining.)

2. Add frosting to cake crumbs; mix with hands until well blended. Shape mixture into 1½-inch balls (about 2 tablespoons cake mixture per ball); place on prepared baking sheet. Cover with plastic wrap; refrigerate at least 1 hour or freeze 10 minutes to firm.

3. Meanwhile, prepare hair. Press and flatten chocolate candies into thin rectangles. (If candies are too stiff to flatten, microwave several seconds to soften.) Use scissors to make ¼-inch-long cuts across bottom (long) edge of candy. Fold candy into thirds or roll up candy so fringe is on top; separate and bend fringe pieces to create hair.

4. When cake balls are firm, place candy coating in deep microwavable bowl. Melt according to package directions. Dip one lollipop stick about ½ inch into melted coating; insert stick into cake ball (no more than halfway through). Return cake pop to baking sheet in refrigerator to set. Repeat with remaining cake balls and sticks.

5. Working with one cake pop at a time, hold stick and dip cake ball into melted coating to cover completely, letting excess coating drip off. Rotate stick gently and/or tap stick on edge of bowl, if necessary, to remove excess coating. Place cake pop in foam block. Immediately attach two chocolate pieces to sides of pop for ears while coating is still wet; hold in place until coating is set.

6. Dip toothpick in candy coating; place dot of coating on cake pops to attach yellow candy. Pipe two dots of black frosting above yellow candy for eyes; pipe smile on yellow candy. Pipe dot of yellow frosting in each ear. Dip toothpick in candy coating; place dot of coating on cake pops to attach hair. Hold in place until coating is set.   *Makes about 24 pops*

Funky Monkeys

Little Ladybugs

½ baked and cooled 13×9-inch cake*
½ cup plus 2 tablespoons frosting
1 package (14 to 16 ounces) red candy coating
24 lollipop sticks
Foam block
Dark chocolate-covered peanuts or other round candies (about ½ inch in diameter)
1½ cups semisweet chocolate chips
White and red decors or small candies
Chocolate sprinkles

Prepare a cake from a mix according to package directions or use your favorite recipe. Cake must be cooled completely.

1. Line large baking sheet with waxed paper. Use hands to crumble cake into large bowl. (You should end up with fine crumbs and no large cake pieces remaining.)

2. Add frosting to cake crumbs; mix with hands until well blended. Shape mixture into 1½-inch balls (about 2 tablespoons cake mixture per ball); place on prepared baking sheet. Cover with plastic wrap; refrigerate at least 1 hour or freeze 10 minutes to firm.

3. When cake balls are firm, place candy coating in deep microwavable bowl. Melt according to package directions. Dip one lollipop stick about ½ inch into melted coating; insert stick into cake ball (no more than halfway through). Return cake pop to baking sheet in refrigerator to set. Repeat with remaining cake balls and sticks.

4. Working with one cake pop at a time, hold stick and dip cake ball into melted coating to cover completely, letting excess coating drip off. Rotate stick gently and/or tap stick on edge of bowl, if necessary, to remove excess coating. Place cake pop in foam block. Immediately attach chocolate-covered candy to front of pop for head while coating is still wet; hold in place until coating is set.

5. Place chocolate chips in small resealable food storage bag. Microwave on MEDIUM (50%) 1 minute. Knead bag; microwave 30 seconds to 1 minute or until chocolate is melted and smooth. Cut off small corner of bag; pipe stripe of chocolate down center of each cake pop starting from head. Pipe small circles of chocolate all over cake pop for ladybug spots.

6. Pipe two very small dots of chocolate (or use toothpick) on candy head; attach white decors for eyes using tweezers. Add dot of chocolate and red decor for mouth. Pipe two dots of chocolate above eyes; attach two chocolate sprinkles vertically for antennae. Pipe tiny dot of chocolate in center of each eye.

Makes about 24 pops

Little Ladybugs

Hoppin' Pops

½ baked and cooled 13×9-inch cake*
½ cup plus 2 tablespoons frosting
½ (14- to 16-ounce) package yellow candy coating
½ (14- to 16-ounce) package pink candy coating
24 lollipop sticks
   Foam block
   Mini semisweet chocolate chips
   White decorator frosting
   Granulated sugar

Prepare a cake from a mix according to package directions or use your favorite recipe. Cake must be cooled completely.

1. Line large baking sheet with waxed paper. Use hands to crumble cake into large bowl. (You should end up with fine crumbs and no large cake pieces remaining.)

2. Add frosting to cake crumbs; mix with hands until well blended. Shape mixture into bunny heads (about 2 tablespoons cake mixture per head); place on prepared baking sheet. Cover with plastic wrap; refrigerate at least 1 hour or freeze 10 minutes to firm.

3. When cake balls are firm, place candy coatings in separate deep microwavable bowls. Melt according to package directions. Dip one lollipop stick about ½ inch into melted coating; insert stick into cake ball (no more than halfway through). Return cake pop to baking sheet in refrigerator to set. Repeat with remaining cake balls and sticks.

4. Working with one cake pop at a time, hold stick and dip cake ball into melted coating to cover completely, letting excess coating drip off. Rotate stick gently and/or tap stick on edge of bowl, if necessary, to remove excess coating. Place cake pop in foam block. Immediately attach two mini chips to pop for eyes while coating is still wet; hold in place until coating is set.

5. Dip toothpick in candy coating; place dot of coating below eyes to attach additional mini chip for nose.

6. Pipe white frosting in center of each ear; sprinkle with sugar to coat. Brush off any excess sugar from cake pops.

Makes about 24 pops

Hoppin' Pops

Teddy Bear Pops

½ baked and cooled 13×9-inch cake*
½ cup plus 2 tablespoons frosting
1 package (14 to 16 ounces) peanut butter candy coating
24 lollipop sticks
Foam block
1½ cups extra-large semisweet chocolate chips, divided
White chocolate chips
Mini semisweet chocolate chips

Prepare a cake from a mix according to package directions or use your favorite recipe. Cake must be cooled completely.

1. Line large baking sheet with waxed paper. Use hands to crumble cake into large bowl. (You should end up with fine crumbs and no large cake pieces remaining.)

2. Add frosting to cake crumbs; mix with hands until well blended. Shape mixture into 1½-inch balls (about 2 tablespoons cake mixture per ball); place on prepared baking sheet. Cover with plastic wrap; refrigerate at least 1 hour or freeze 10 minutes to firm.

3. When cake balls are firm, place candy coating in deep microwavable bowl. Melt according to package directions. Dip one lollipop stick about ½ inch into melted coating; insert stick into cake ball (no more than halfway through). Return cake pop to baking sheet in refrigerator to set. Repeat with remaining cake balls and sticks.

4. Working with one cake pop at a time, hold stick and dip cake ball into melted coating to cover completely, letting excess coating drip off. Rotate stick gently and/or tap stick on edge of bowl, if necessary, to remove excess coating. Place cake pop in foam block. Immediately attach two large chocolate chips to top of pop for ears while coating is still wet; hold in place until coating is set.

5. Dip toothpick in candy coating; place two dots of coating on cake pops to attach white chips for eyes. Add dot of coating and mini chocolate chip for nose.

6. When all pops have ears, eyes and noses, place remaining large chocolate chips in small resealable food storage bag. Microwave on MEDIUM (50%) 45 seconds. Knead bag; microwave 30 seconds to 1 minute or until chocolate is melted and smooth. Cut off small corner of bag; pipe mouths and pupils on bear faces.

Makes about 24 pops

Teddy Bear Pops

Busy Bees

½ baked and cooled 13×9-inch cake*
½ cup plus 2 tablespoons frosting
1 package (14 to 16 ounces) yellow candy coating
24 lollipop sticks
Foam block
Black decorator frosting
Black string licorice, cut into ¾-inch lengths

*Prepare a cake from a mix according to package directions or use your favorite recipe. Cake must be cooled completely.

1. Line large baking sheet with waxed paper. Use hands to crumble cake into large bowl. (You should end up with fine crumbs and no large cake pieces remaining.)

2. Add frosting to cake crumbs; mix with hands until well blended. Shape mixture into 1½-inch balls (about 2 tablespoons cake mixture per ball); place on prepared baking sheet. Cover with plastic wrap; refrigerate at least 1 hour or freeze 10 minutes to firm.

3. Reserve 24 yellow candy coating discs for wings. Cut reserved discs in half, then cut small piece from each half to create flat edge.

4. When cake balls are firm, place remaining yellow candy coating in deep microwavable bowl. Melt according to package directions. Dip one lollipop stick about ½ inch into melted coating; insert stick into cake ball (no more than halfway through). Return cake pop to baking sheet in refrigerator to set. Repeat with remaining cake balls and sticks.

5. Working with one cake pop at a time, hold stick and dip cake ball into melted coating to cover completely, letting excess coating drip off. Rotate stick gently and/or tap stick on edge of bowl, if necessary, to remove excess coating. Place cake pop in foam block.

6. Pipe three stripes of black frosting around each cake pop. Dip toothpick in candy coating; place two dots of coating behind center stripe. Press reserved yellow disc halves, flat sides facing you, into coating for wings; hold in place until coating is set.

7. Pipe two dots of frosting at top of first stripe; attach two licorice pieces for antennae and hold in place until set. Pipe eyes and smile with black frosting. *Makes about 24 pops*

Busy Bees

Playtime Pops

Home Run Pops

½ baked and cooled 13×9-inch cake*
½ cup plus 2 tablespoons frosting
1 package (14 to 16 ounces) white candy coating
24 lollipop sticks
Foam block
Red decorator frosting

Prepare a cake from a mix according to package directions or use your favorite recipe. Cake must be cooled completely.

1. Line large baking sheet with waxed paper. Use hands to crumble cake into large bowl. (You should end up with fine crumbs and no large cake pieces remaining.)

2. Add frosting to cake crumbs; mix with hands until well blended. Shape mixture into 1½-inch balls (about 2 tablespoons cake mixture per ball); place on prepared baking sheet. Cover with plastic wrap; refrigerate at least 1 hour or freeze 10 minutes to firm.

3. When cake balls are firm, place candy coating in deep microwavable bowl. Melt according to package directions. Dip one lollipop stick about ½ inch into melted coating; insert stick into cake ball (no more than halfway through). Return cake pop to baking sheet in refrigerator to set. Repeat with remaining cake balls and sticks.

4. Working with one cake pop at a time, hold stick and dip cake ball into melted coating to cover completely, letting excess coating drip off. Rotate stick gently and/or tap stick on edge of bowl, if necessary, to remove excess coating. Place cake pop in foam block.

5. Pipe seams on cake pops with red frosting.   *Makes about 24 pops*

Tiny Taffy Apples

½ baked and cooled 13×9-inch cake*
½ cup plus 2 tablespoons frosting
1 package (14 to 16 ounces) peanut butter candy coating
24 lollipop sticks
2 cups chopped peanuts
24 paper baking cups (optional)

Prepare a cake from a mix according to package directions or use your favorite recipe. Cake must be cooled completely.

1. Line large baking sheet with waxed paper. Use hands to crumble cake into large bowl. (You should end up with fine crumbs and no large cake pieces remaining.)

2. Add frosting to cake crumbs; mix with hands until well blended. Shape mixture into 1½-inch balls (about 2 tablespoons cake mixture per ball); place on prepared baking sheet. Cover with plastic wrap; refrigerate at least 1 hour or freeze 10 minutes to firm.

3. When cake balls are firm, place candy coating in deep microwavable bowl. Melt according to package directions. Dip one lollipop stick about ½ inch into melted coating; insert stick into cake ball (no more than halfway through). Return cake pop to baking sheet in refrigerator to set. Repeat with remaining cake balls and sticks.

4. Place peanuts in shallow bowl. Working with one cake pop at a time, hold stick and dip cake ball into melted coating to cover completely, letting excess coating drip off. Rotate stick gently and/or tap stick on edge of bowl, if necessary, to remove excess coating.

5. Immediately roll cake pop in peanuts to coat bottom half or three fourths of pop; press peanuts in gently to adhere to coating. Place cake pops in baking cups, if desired.

Makes about 24 pops

Tiny Taffy Apples

Balloon Pops

½ baked and cooled 13×9-inch cake*
½ cup plus 2 tablespoons frosting
    Red, yellow or blue chewy fruit candy squares or taffy strips
1 package (14 to 16 ounces) red, yellow or blue candy coating
24 lollipop sticks
    Foam block

Prepare a cake from a mix according to package directions or use your favorite recipe. Cake must be cooled completely.

1. Line large baking sheet with waxed paper. Use hands to crumble cake into large bowl. (You should end up with fine crumbs and no large cake pieces remaining.)

2. Add frosting to cake crumbs; mix with hands until well blended. Shape mixture into 1½-inch balls (about 2 tablespoons cake mixture per ball); place on prepared baking sheet. Cover with plastic wrap; refrigerate at least 1 hour or freeze 10 minutes to firm.

3. Meanwhile, prepare balloon knots. Unwrap candy squares; cut each into four pieces. Working with one piece at a time, microwave on LOW (30%) 5 seconds or until softened. Press candy between hands or on waxed paper to flatten and shape into ⅛-inch-thick circle. Use end of lollipop stick to poke hole in center of circle; bend circle into cone shape to resemble balloon knot.

4. When cake balls are firm, place candy coating in deep microwavable bowl. Melt according to package directions. Dip one lollipop stick about ½ inch into melted coating; insert stick into cake ball (no more than halfway through). Return cake pop to baking sheet in refrigerator to set. Repeat with remaining cake balls and sticks.

5. Working with one cake pop at a time, hold stick and dip cake ball into melted coating to cover completely, letting excess coating drip off. Rotate stick gently and/or tap stick on edge of bowl, if necessary, to remove excess coating. Place cake pop in foam block.

6. Dip toothpick in candy coating; place dots of coating around base of each cake pop where stick is attached. Slide candy balloon knot up stick and attach to base of cake pop; hold in place until coating is set.

Makes about 24 pops

Balloon Pops

Touchdown Treats

½ baked and cooled 13×9-inch cake*
½ cup plus 2 tablespoons frosting
 1 package (14 to 16 ounces) chocolate candy coating
24 lollipop sticks
   Foam block
   White decorator frosting

Prepare a cake from a mix according to package directions or use your favorite recipe. Cake must be cooled completely.

1. Line large baking sheet with waxed paper. Use hands to crumble cake into large bowl. (You should end up with fine crumbs and no large cake pieces remaining.)

2. Add frosting to cake crumbs; mix with hands until well blended. Shape mixture into tapered oval footballs (about 2 tablespoons cake mixture per football); place on prepared baking sheet. Cover with plastic wrap; refrigerate at least 1 hour or freeze 10 minutes to firm.

3. When cake balls are firm, place candy coating in deep microwavable bowl. Melt according to package directions. Dip one lollipop stick about ½ inch into melted coating; insert stick into cake ball (no more than halfway through). Return cake pop to baking sheet in refrigerator to set. Repeat with remaining cake balls and sticks.

4. Working with one cake pop at a time, hold stick and dip cake ball into melted coating to cover completely, letting excess coating drip off. Rotate stick gently and/or tap stick on edge of bowl, if necessary, to remove excess coating. Place cake pop in foam block.

5. Pipe laces and lines on cake pops with white frosting.   *Makes about 24 pops*

Touchdown Treats

Sweet Swirly Pops

½ baked and cooled 13×9-inch cake*
½ cup plus 2 tablespoons frosting
½ (14- to 16-ounce) package chocolate candy coating
½ (14- to 16-ounce) package white candy coating
½ (14- to 16-ounce) package pink and/or red candy coating
24 lollipop sticks
   Foam block

*Prepare a cake from a mix according to package directions or use your favorite recipe. Cake must be cooled completely.

1. Line large baking sheet with waxed paper. Use hands to crumble cake into large bowl. (You should end up with fine crumbs and no large cake pieces remaining.)

2. Add frosting to cake crumbs; mix with hands until well blended. Shape mixture into 1½-inch balls (about 2 tablespoons cake mixture per ball); place on prepared baking sheet. Cover with plastic wrap; refrigerate at least 1 hour or freeze 10 minutes to firm.

3. When cake balls are firm, place candy coatings in separate deep microwavable bowls. Melt according to package directions. Dip one lollipop stick about ½ inch into melted coating; insert stick into cake ball (no more than halfway through). Return cake pop to baking sheet in refrigerator to set. Repeat with remaining cake balls and sticks.

4. Working with one cake pop at a time, hold stick and dip cake ball into melted chocolate or white coating to cover completely, letting excess coating drip off. Rotate stick gently and/or tap stick on edge of bowl, if necessary, to remove excess coating.

5. Immediately drizzle cake pop with melted pink or red coating using fork or spoon, turning pop constantly while drizzling. (For swirls to set smoothly in base coating, pop must be turned or shaken while drizzling, and drizzling must be done while base coating is still wet.) Place cake pop in foam block to set.   *Makes about 24 pops*

Tip: To make cake pops with two color swirls, drizzle cake pop with both colors immediately after dipping in base coating as directed in step 5.

Sweet Swirly Pops

Lucky Dice Pops

½ baked and cooled 13×9-inch cake*
½ cup plus 2 tablespoons frosting
 1 package (14 to 16 ounces) white candy coating
24 lollipop sticks
　 Foam block
　 Black decorator frosting or black gel frosting

Prepare a cake from a mix according to package directions or use your favorite recipe. Cake must be cooled completely.

1. Line large baking sheet with waxed paper. Use hands to crumble cake into large bowl. (You should end up with fine crumbs and no large cake pieces remaining.)

2. Add frosting to cake crumbs; mix with hands until well blended. Shape mixture into 1½-inch balls (about 2 tablespoons cake mixture per ball); shape balls into squares. Place on prepared baking sheet. Cover with plastic wrap; refrigerate at least 1 hour or freeze 10 minutes to firm.

3. When cake balls are firm, place candy coating in deep microwavable bowl. Melt according to package directions. Dip one lollipop stick about ½ inch into melted coating; insert stick into cake ball (no more than halfway through). Return cake pop to baking sheet in refrigerator to set. Repeat with remaining cake balls and sticks.

4. Working with one cake pop at a time, hold stick and dip cake ball into melted coating to cover completely, letting excess coating drip off. Rotate stick gently and/or tap stick on edge of bowl, if necessary, to remove excess coating. Place cake pop in foam block.

5. Pipe dots on top and sides of cake pops with black frosting. *Makes about 24 pops*

Lucky Dice Pops

Pretty Package Pops

½ baked and cooled 13×9-inch cake*
½ cup plus 2 tablespoons frosting
½ (14- to 16-ounce) package blue candy coating
½ (14- to 16-ounce) package purple candy coating
24 lollipop sticks
   Foam block
   Assorted color taffy and gummy strips
   Assorted color spice drops or gumdrops

Prepare a cake from a mix according to package directions or use your favorite recipe. Cake must be cooled completely.

1. Line large baking sheet with waxed paper. Use hands to crumble cake into large bowl. (You should end up with fine crumbs and no large cake pieces remaining.)

2. Add frosting to cake crumbs; mix with hands until well blended. Shape mixture into 1½-inch balls (about 2 tablespoons cake mixture per ball); shape balls into squares. Place on prepared baking sheet. Cover with plastic wrap; refrigerate at least 1 hour or freeze 10 minutes to firm.

3. When cake balls are firm, place candy coatings in separate deep microwavable bowls. Melt according to package directions. Dip one lollipop stick about ½ inch into melted coating; insert stick into cake ball (no more than halfway through). Return cake pop to baking sheet in refrigerator to set. Repeat with remaining cake balls and sticks.

4. Working with one cake pop at a time, hold stick and dip cake ball into melted coating to cover completely, letting excess coating drip off. Rotate stick gently and/or tap stick on edge of bowl, if necessary, to remove excess coating. Place cake pop in foam block.

5. Cut pieces of taffy or gummy strips with scissors to fit around cake pops for ribbons. Apply coating to back of each taffy piece with toothpick; press onto cake pops and hold until coating is set.

6. For candy bows, cut slits in top of spice drops (cut about halfway through candies). Separate cut pieces of spice drops, pressing them outward to resemble loops of bow. (For bigger bow, cut small pieces from additional spice drop and press them into center of bow.) Dip toothpick in candy coating; place dot of coating on top of cake pops to attach bows.

Makes about 24 pops

Tip: Instead of using taffy and spice drops, you can pipe decorator frosting around and on top of the cake pops to resemble ribbons and bows.

·Playtime Pops·

Pretty Package Pops

Spicy Chocolate Pops

½ baked and cooled 13×9-inch chocolate cake* (see Tip)
½ cup plus 2 tablespoons frosting
1 package (14 to 16 ounces) chocolate candy coating
24 lollipop sticks
Ground red pepper
Ground cinnamon
Foam block

Prepare a cake from a mix according to package directions or use your favorite recipe. Cake must be cooled completely.

1. Line large baking sheet with waxed paper. Use hands to crumble cake into large bowl. (You should end up with fine crumbs and no large cake pieces remaining.)

2. Add frosting to cake crumbs; mix with hands until well blended. Shape mixture into 1½-inch balls (about 2 tablespoons cake mixture per ball); place on prepared baking sheet. Cover with plastic wrap; refrigerate at least 1 hour or freeze 10 minutes to firm.

3. When cake balls are firm, place candy coating in deep microwavable bowl. Melt according to package directions. Dip one lollipop stick about ½ inch into melted coating; insert stick into cake ball (no more than halfway through). Return cake pop to baking sheet in refrigerator to set. Repeat with remaining cake balls and sticks.

4. Working with one cake pop at a time, hold stick and dip cake ball into melted coating to cover completely, letting excess coating drip off. Rotate stick gently and/or tap stick on edge of bowl, if necessary, to remove excess coating.

5. Immediately sprinkle cake pop lightly with red pepper and cinnamon while coating is still wet. Place cake pop in foam block to set. *Makes about 24 pops*

Tip: For more spicy chocolate flavor, add 1 teaspoon ground cinnamon and ¼ to ½ teaspoon ground red pepper to the batter when preparing your chocolate cake.

Spicy Chocolate Pops

High-Flying Kites

½ baked and cooled 13×9-inch cake*
½ cup plus 2 tablespoons frosting
½ (14- to 16-ounce) package purple candy coating
½ (14- to 16-ounce) package green candy coating
24 lollipop sticks
   Foam block
   Yellow decorator frosting
   Assorted color decors and small candies
   Yellow string licorice

Prepare a cake from a mix according to package directions or use your favorite recipe. Cake must be cooled completely.

1. Line large baking sheet with waxed paper. Use hands to crumble cake into large bowl. (You should end up with fine crumbs and no large cake pieces remaining.)

2. Add frosting to cake crumbs; mix with hands until well blended. Shape mixture into 1½-inch balls (about 2 tablespoons cake mixture per ball); shape balls into diamonds. Place on prepared baking sheet. Cover with plastic wrap; refrigerate at least 1 hour or freeze 10 minutes to firm.

3. When cake balls are firm, place candy coatings in separate deep microwavable bowls. Melt according to package directions. Dip one lollipop stick about ½ inch into melted coating; insert stick into cake ball (no more than halfway through). Return cake pop to baking sheet in refrigerator to set. Repeat with remaining cake balls and sticks.

4. Working with one cake pop at a time, hold stick and dip cake ball into melted coating to cover completely, letting excess coating drip off. Rotate stick gently and/or tap stick on edge of bowl, if necessary, to remove excess coating. Place cake pop in foam block.

5. Pipe crossbars on cake pops with yellow frosting. Dip toothpick in candy coating; place dots of coating on cake pops to attach decors and candies.

6. Cut licorice into desired lengths for kite tails. Attach licorice to back of cake pops with coating; hold in place until coating is set.

Makes about 24 pops

High-Flying Kites

Party Poppers

½ baked and cooled 13×9-inch cake*
½ cup plus 2 tablespoons frosting
½ (14- to 16-ounce) package blue candy coating
½ (14- to 16-ounce) package red candy coating
24 lollipop sticks
   Foam block
   Red and blue gumdrops or other round candies
   Red and blue decorator frosting
   Red, white and blue sprinkles and decors

Prepare a cake from a mix according to package directions or use your favorite recipe. Cake must be cooled completely.

1. Line large baking sheet with waxed paper. Use hands to crumble cake into large bowl. (You should end up with fine crumbs and no large cake pieces remaining.)

2. Add frosting to cake crumbs; mix with hands until well blended. Shape mixture into 2½-inch-tall triangles (about 2 tablespoons cake mixture per triangle); place on prepared baking sheet. Cover with plastic wrap; refrigerate at least 1 hour or freeze 10 minutes to firm.

3. When cake balls are firm, place candy coatings in separate deep microwavable bowls. Melt according to package directions. Dip one lollipop stick about ½ inch into melted coating; insert stick into cake ball (no more than halfway through). Return cake pop to baking sheet in refrigerator to set. Repeat with remaining cake balls and sticks.

4. Working with one cake pop at a time, hold stick and dip cake ball into melted coating to cover completely, letting excess coating drip off. Rotate stick gently and/or tap stick on edge of bowl, if necessary, to remove excess coating. Place cake pop in foam block. Immediately attach gumdrop to top of pop while coating is still wet; hold in place until coating is set.

5. Pipe decorator frosting along bottom of each cake pop. Pipe dots on cake pops with frosting, or dip toothpick in candy coating and place dots of coating on cake pops to attach sprinkles and decors.

Makes about 24 pops

Party Poppers

Holiday Pops

Sweetheart Pops

½ baked and cooled 13×9-inch cake*
½ cup plus 2 tablespoons frosting
 1 package (14 to 16 ounces) pink candy coating
24 lollipop sticks
   Foam block
   White decors, sugar pearls or sprinkles

Prepare a cake from a mix according to package directions or use your favorite recipe. Cake must be cooled completely.

1. Line large baking sheet with waxed paper. Use hands to crumble cake into large bowl. (You should end up with fine crumbs and no large cake pieces remaining.)

2. Add frosting to cake crumbs; mix with hands until well blended. Shape mixture into 1½-inch-balls (about 2 tablespoons cake mixture per ball); shape balls into hearts. Place on prepared baking sheet. Cover with plastic wrap; refrigerate at least 1 hour or freeze 10 minutes to firm.

3. When cake balls are firm, place candy coating in deep microwavable bowl. Melt according to package directions. Dip one lollipop stick about ½ inch into melted coating; insert stick into cake ball (no more than halfway through). Return cake pop to baking sheet in refrigerator to set. Repeat with remaining cake balls and sticks.

4. Working with one cake pop at a time, hold stick and dip cake ball into melted coating to cover completely, letting excess coating drip off. Rotate stick gently and/or tap stick on edge of bowl, if necessary, to remove excess coating. Place cake pop in foam block.

5. Dip toothpick in candy coating; place dots of coating on cake pops to attach decors and sugar pearls.

Makes about 24 pops

Variation: For quicker decorating, use white decorator frosting instead of decors. Pipe dots, hearts or lines on cake pops as desired.

Earth Pops

½ baked and cooled 13×9-inch cake*
½ cup plus 2 tablespoons frosting
1 package (14 to 16 ounces) blue candy coating
½ package (14 to 16 ounces) green candy coating
24 lollipop sticks
Foam block

Prepare a cake from a mix according to package directions or use your favorite recipe. Cake must be cooled completely.

1. Line large baking sheet with waxed paper. Use hands to crumble cake into large bowl. (You should end up with fine crumbs and no large cake pieces remaining.)

2. Add frosting to cake crumbs; mix with hands until well blended. Shape mixture into 1½-inch balls (about 2 tablespoons cake mixture per ball); place on prepared baking sheet. Cover with plastic wrap; refrigerate at least 1 hour or freeze 10 minutes to firm.

3. When cake balls are firm, place candy coatings in separate deep microwavable bowls. Melt according to package directions. Dip one lollipop stick about ½ inch into melted blue coating; insert stick into cake ball (no more than halfway through). Return cake pop to baking sheet in refrigerator to set. Repeat with remaining cake balls and sticks.

4. Working with one cake pop at a time, hold stick and dip cake ball into melted blue coating to cover completely, letting excess coating drip off. Rotate stick gently and/or tap stick on edge of bowl, if necessary, to remove excess coating.

5. Immediately drizzle cake pop with melted green coating using fork or spoon, turning pop constantly while drizzling. (For green swirls to set smoothly in blue coating, pop must be turned or shaken while drizzling, and drizzling must be done while blue coating is still wet.) Place cake pop in foam block to set.

Makes about 24 pops

Earth Pops

Easter Egg Pops

½ baked and cooled 13×9-inch cake*
½ cup plus 2 tablespoons frosting
½ (14- to 16-ounce) package pink candy coating
½ (14- to 16-ounce) package yellow candy coating
24 lollipop sticks
   Foam block
   White, yellow and pink decorator frosting
   Pastel-colored decors, sugar pearls or sprinkles

*Prepare a cake from a mix according to package directions or use your favorite recipe. Cake must be cooled completely.

1. Line large baking sheet with waxed paper. Use hands to crumble cake into large bowl. (You should end up with fine crumbs and no large cake pieces remaining.)

2. Add frosting to cake crumbs; mix with hands until well blended. Shape mixture into 1½-inch eggs (about 2 tablespoons cake mixture per egg); place on prepared baking sheet. Cover with plastic wrap; refrigerate at least 1 hour or freeze 10 minutes to firm.

3. When cake balls are firm, place candy coatings in separate deep microwavable bowls. Melt according to package directions. Dip one lollipop stick about ½ inch into melted coating; insert stick into cake ball (no more than halfway through). Return cake pop to baking sheet in refrigerator to set. Repeat with remaining cake balls and sticks.

4. Working with one cake pop at a time, hold stick and dip cake ball into melted coating to cover completely, letting excess coating drip off. Rotate stick gently and/or tap stick on edge of bowl, if necessary, to remove excess coating. Place cake pop in foam block.

5. Pipe lines on cake pops with decorator frosting. Dip toothpick in candy coating; place dots of coating on cake pops to attach decors and sugar pearls.

Makes about 24 pops

Easter Egg Pops

Easy Easter Pops

½ baked and cooled 13×9-inch cake*
½ cup plus 2 tablespoons frosting
½ (14- to 16-ounce) package yellow candy coating
½ (14- to 16-ounce) package purple candy coating
24 lollipop sticks
   Foam block

Prepare a cake from a mix according to package directions or use your favorite recipe. Cake must be cooled completely.

1. Line large baking sheet with waxed paper. Use hands to crumble cake into large bowl. (You should end up with fine crumbs and no large cake pieces remaining.)

2. Add frosting to cake crumbs; mix with hands until well blended. Shape mixture into 1½-inch balls (about 2 tablespoons cake mixture per ball); place on prepared baking sheet. Cover with plastic wrap; refrigerate at least 1 hour or freeze 10 minutes to firm.

3. When cake balls are firm, place candy coatings in separate deep microwavable bowls. Melt according to package directions. Dip one lollipop stick about ½ inch into melted coating; insert stick into cake ball (no more than halfway through). Return cake pop to baking sheet in refrigerator to set. Repeat with remaining cake balls and sticks.

4. Working with one cake pop at a time, hold stick and dip cake ball into melted coating to cover completely, letting excess coating drip off. Rotate stick gently and/or tap stick on edge of bowl, if necessary, to remove excess coating. Place cake pop in foam block to set.

5. Transfer remaining candy coatings to two small resealable food storage bags. (Reheat briefly in microwave if coatings have hardened.) Cut off small corner of each bag; drizzle pops with contrasting color coating.
Makes about 24 pops

Easy Easter Pops

Boo Bites

½ baked and cooled 13×9-inch cake*
½ cup plus 2 tablespoons frosting
1 package (14 to 16 ounces) white candy coating
24 lollipop sticks
Foam block
Black decorator frosting or black gel frosting

*Prepare a cake from a mix according to package directions or use your favorite recipe. Cake must be cooled completely.

1. Line large baking sheet with waxed paper. Use hands to crumble cake into large bowl. (You should end up with fine crumbs and no large cake pieces remaining.)

2. Add frosting to cake crumbs; mix with hands until well blended. Shape mixture into rounded triangles (about 2 tablespoons cake mixture per triangle), about 2 inches tall and with uneven or wavy edges to resemble ghosts. Place on prepared baking sheet. Cover with plastic wrap; refrigerate at least 1 hour or freeze 10 minutes to firm.

3. When cake balls are firm, place candy coating in deep microwavable bowl. Melt according to package directions. Dip one lollipop stick about ½ inch into melted coating; insert stick into cake ball (no more than halfway through). Return cake pop to baking sheet in refrigerator to set. Repeat with remaining cake balls and sticks.

4. Working with one cake pop at a time, hold stick and dip cake ball into melted coating to cover completely, letting excess coating drip off. Rotate stick gently and/or tap stick on edge of bowl, if necessary, to remove excess coating. Place cake pop in foam block.

5. Pipe eyes and mouths on cake pops with black frosting.   *Makes about 24 pops*

Boo Bites

Pumpkin Patch Pops

½ baked and cooled 13×9-inch cake*
½ cup plus 2 tablespoons frosting
1½ packages (14 to 16 ounces each) orange candy coating
24 lollipop sticks
 Green gumdrops or spice drops
 Foam block

*Prepare a cake from a mix according to package directions or use your favorite recipe. Cake must be cooled completely.

1. Line large baking sheet with waxed paper. Use hands to crumble cake into large bowl. (You should end up with fine crumbs and no large cake pieces remaining.)

2. Add frosting to cake crumbs; mix with hands until well blended. Shape mixture into 1½-inch balls (about 2 tablespoons cake mixture per ball); flatten balls slightly to resemble pumpkin shape and make indentation in top of each ball for stem. Place on prepared baking sheet. Cover with plastic wrap; refrigerate at least 1 hour or freeze 10 minutes to firm.

3. When cake balls are firm, place candy coating in deep microwavable bowl. Melt according to package directions. Dip one lollipop stick about ½ inch into melted coating; insert stick into cake ball (no more than halfway through). Return cake pop to baking sheet in refrigerator to set. Repeat with remaining cake balls and sticks.

4. Cut gumdrops in half, if necessary, to create stems. Working with one cake pop at a time, hold stick and dip cake ball into melted coating to cover completely, letting excess coating drip off. Rotate stick gently and/or tap stick on edge of bowl, if necessary, to remove excess coating. Place cake pop in foam block. Immediately attach gumdrop to top of pop while coating is still wet; hold in place until coating is set.

5. Transfer remaining candy coating to small resealable food storage bag. (Reheat briefly in microwave if coating has hardened.) Cut off small corner of bag; pipe vertical lines on each cake pop from stem to stick. Pipe coating around stem, if desired.   *Makes about 24 pops*

Variation: You can use orange decorator frosting instead of the candy coating to pipe the lines on the cake pops.

Pumpkin Patch Pops

Reindeer Pops

½ baked and cooled 13×9-inch cake*
½ cup plus 2 tablespoons frosting
1 package (14 to 16 ounces) chocolate candy coating
24 lollipop sticks
48 small pretzel twists
    Foam block
    Semisweet chocolate chips
    Round white candies
    Red candy-coated chocolate pieces
    Black decorator frosting or black gel frosting

*Prepare a cake from a mix according to package directions or use your favorite recipe. Cake must be cooled completely.

1. Line large baking sheet with waxed paper. Use hands to crumble cake into large bowl. (You should end up with fine crumbs and no large cake pieces remaining.)

2. Add frosting to cake crumbs; mix with hands until well blended. Shape mixture into rounded triangles or skull shape (about 2 tablespoons cake mixture per triangle); place on prepared baking sheet. Cover with plastic wrap; refrigerate at least 1 hour or freeze 10 minutes to firm.

3. When cake balls are firm, place candy coating in deep microwavable bowl. Melt according to package directions. Dip one lollipop stick about ½ inch into melted coating; insert stick into cake ball (no more than halfway through). Return cake pop to baking sheet in refrigerator to set. Repeat with remaining cake balls and sticks.

4. Break off one section from each pretzel twist; set aside.

5. Working with one cake pop at a time, hold stick and dip cake ball into melted coating to cover completely, letting excess coating drip off. Rotate stick gently and/or tap stick on edge of bowl, if necessary, to remove excess coating. Place cake pop in foam block. Immediately attach two pretzel twists to top of pop for antlers while coating is still wet; hold in place until coating is set.

6. Dip toothpick in candy coating; place two dots of coating on either side of pretzel twists to attach chocolate chips for ears. Add two dots of coating and white candies for eyes. Add dot of coating and chocolate piece for nose. Pipe dot of black frosting in center of each eye.

Makes about 24 pops

Reindeer Pops

Frosty's Friends

½ baked and cooled 13×9-inch cake*
½ cup plus 2 tablespoons frosting
 1 package (14 to 16 ounces) white candy coating
16 lollipop sticks
   Foam block
   Orange candy-coated sunflower seeds or chocolate pieces
   Assorted color decors and candy dots
   Black decorator frosting or black gel frosting
   Assorted color taffy, gummy strings or string licorice
   Assorted color gumdrops, candy discs and chocolate kisses

*Prepare a cake from a mix according to package directions or use your favorite recipe. Cake must be cooled completely.

1. Line large baking sheet with waxed paper. Use hands to crumble cake into large bowl. (You should end up with fine crumbs and no large cake pieces remaining.)

2. Add frosting to cake crumbs; mix with hands until well blended. Shape mixture into 24 (1½-inch) balls (about 2 tablespoons cake mixture per ball); place 16 balls on prepared baking sheet. Divide each of remaining 8 balls in half; shape into smaller balls for heads and place on baking sheet. Cover with plastic wrap; refrigerate at least 1 hour or freeze 10 minutes to firm.

3. When cake balls are firm, place candy coating in deep microwavable bowl. Melt according to package directions. Dip one lollipop stick about 1 inch into melted coating; insert stick through larger cake ball so ½ inch of stick comes out top of cake ball. Dip end of stick in melted coating again; insert stick into smaller cake ball to create snowman head. (Cake balls should be touching.) Return cake pop to baking sheet in refrigerator to set. Repeat with remaining cake balls and sticks.

4. Working with one cake pop at a time, hold stick and dip cake balls into melted coating to cover completely, letting excess coating drip off. Rotate stick gently and/or tap stick on edge of bowl, if necessary, to remove excess coating. Place cake pop in foam block.

5. Cut orange candies in half for noses. Dip toothpick in candy coating; place dot of coating on cake pops to attach candy nose. Attach decors to snowman bodies for buttons. Pipe eyes and mouths with black frosting. Cut or stretch taffy or gummy strings into long thin pieces for scarves. Carefully tie scarves around snowman necks. Create hats using candies, decors and licorice. Attach hats with dots of coating.

Makes about 16 pops

·Holiday Pops·

Frosty's Friends

Jolly Pops

½ baked and cooled 13×9-inch cake*
½ cup plus 2 tablespoons frosting
1 package (14 to 16 ounces) red candy coating
24 lollipop sticks
    Foam block
    White candies, gumdrops or mini marshmallows
    White decorator frosting

*Prepare a cake from a mix according to package directions or use your favorite recipe. Cake must be cooled completely.

1. Line large baking sheet with waxed paper. Use hands to crumble cake into large bowl. (You should end up with fine crumbs and no large cake pieces remaining.)

2. Add frosting to cake crumbs; mix with hands until well blended. Shape mixture into 2½-inch-tall triangles (about 2 tablespoons cake mixture per triangle); place on prepared baking sheet. Cover with plastic wrap; refrigerate at least 1 hour or freeze 10 minutes to firm.

3. When cake balls are firm, place candy coating in deep microwavable bowl. Melt according to package directions. Dip one lollipop stick about ½ inch into melted coating; insert stick into cake ball (no more than halfway through). Return cake pop to baking sheet in refrigerator to set. Repeat with remaining cake balls and sticks.

4. Working with one cake pop at a time, hold stick and dip cake ball into melted coating to cover completely, letting excess coating drip off. Rotate stick gently and/or tap stick on edge of bowl, if necessary, to remove excess coating. Place cake pop in foam block. Immediately attach candy to top of pop while coating is still wet; hold in place until coating is set.

5. Pipe white frosting along bottom of each cake pop.   *Makes about 24 pops*

Jolly Pops

Ornament Pops

½ baked and cooled 13×9-inch cake*
½ cup plus 2 tablespoons frosting
1 package (14 to 16 ounces) white candy coating
24 lollipop sticks
Foam block
Red or yellow string licorice, cut into 1½-inch lengths
Red and green gumdrops or gummy candies
Assorted color candies, sprinkles, decors, sugar pearls and sparkling sugar
Red, white and green decorator frosting

Prepare a cake from a mix according to package directions or use your favorite recipe. Cake must be cooled completely.

1. Line large baking sheet with waxed paper. Use hands to crumble cake into large bowl. (You should end up with fine crumbs and no large cake pieces remaining.)

2. Add frosting to cake crumbs; mix with hands until well blended. Shape mixture into 1½-inch balls (about 2 tablespoons cake mixture per ball); place on prepared baking sheet. Cover with plastic wrap; refrigerate at least 1 hour or freeze 10 minutes to firm.

3. When cake balls are firm, place candy coating in deep microwavable bowl. Melt according to package directions. Dip one lollipop stick about ½ inch into melted coating; insert stick into cake ball (no more than halfway through). Return cake pop to baking sheet in refrigerator to set. Repeat with remaining cake balls and sticks.

4. Working with one cake pop at a time, hold stick and dip cake ball into melted coating to cover completely, letting excess coating drip off. Rotate stick gently and/or tap stick on edge of bowl, if necessary, to remove excess coating. Place cake pop in foam block. Immediately push both ends of licorice piece into top of pop to form hanger while coating is still wet; hold in place until coating is set. (Or press gumdrop or other candy into top of pop.)

5. Decorate cake pops with candies, sprinkles, decors, sugar pearls and sugar, using coating to attach decorations. Pipe lines on cake pops with decorator frosting.

Makes about 24 pops

Ornament Pops

Christmas Tree Pops

½ baked and cooled 13×9-inch cake*
½ cup plus 2 tablespoons frosting
 1 package (14 to 16 ounces) green candy coating
24 lollipop sticks
   Foam block
   White candy stars
   Yellow and white decorator frosting

*Prepare a cake from a mix according to package directions or use your favorite recipe. Cake must be cooled completely.

1. Line large baking sheet with waxed paper. Use hands to crumble cake into large bowl. (You should end up with fine crumbs and no large cake pieces remaining.)

2. Add frosting to cake crumbs; mix with hands until well blended. Shape mixture into 2½-inch-tall triangles (about 2 tablespoons cake mixture per triangle); place on prepared baking sheet. Cover with plastic wrap; refrigerate at least 1 hour or freeze 10 minutes to firm.

3. When cake balls are firm, place candy coating in deep microwavable bowl. Melt according to package directions. Dip one lollipop stick about ½ inch into melted coating; insert stick into cake ball (no more than halfway through). Return cake pop to baking sheet in refrigerator to set. Repeat with remaining cake balls and sticks.

4. Working with one cake pop at a time, hold stick and dip cake ball into melted coating to cover completely, letting excess coating drip off. Rotate stick gently and/or tap stick on edge of bowl, if necessary, to remove excess coating. Place cake pop in foam block. Immediately attach candy star to top of pop while coating is still wet; hold in place until coating is set.

5. Pipe dots on cake pops with decorator frosting.   *Makes about 24 pops*

Christmas Tree Pops

Cookie Jar Jumble

Little Oatmeal Cookies

¾ cup all-purpose flour
½ teaspoon baking soda
½ teaspoon ground cinnamon
¼ teaspoon salt
½ cup (1 stick) butter, softened
½ cup packed brown sugar
¼ cup granulated sugar
1 egg
1 teaspoon vanilla
1½ cups quick or old-fashioned oats
½ cup raisins

1. Preheat oven to 350°F. Whisk flour, baking soda, cinnamon and salt in small bowl.

2. Beat butter, brown sugar and granulated sugar in large bowl with electric mixer at medium speed until creamy. Add egg and vanilla; beat until well blended. Gradually beat in flour mixture at low speed until well blended. Stir in oats and raisins until blended. Drop dough by scant teaspoonfuls 2 inches apart onto ungreased cookie sheets.

3. Bake 8 minutes or just until edges are lightly browned. Cool on cookie sheets 1 minute. Remove to wire racks; cool completely.

Makes about 6 dozen cookies

Chocolate-Topped Linzer Cookies

3 cups hazelnuts, toasted, skins removed, divided
1 cup (2 sticks) butter, softened
1 cup powdered sugar, sifted
½ teaspoon grated lemon peel
¼ teaspoon salt
½ egg*
3 cups sifted all-purpose flour
½ cup nougat paste**
½ cup raspberry jam
6 squares (1 ounce each) semisweet chocolate
2 tablespoons shortening

To measure ½ egg, lightly beat 1 egg in glass measuring cup; remove half for use in recipe.

**Nougat paste, a mixture of ground hazelnuts, sugar and semisweet chocolate, is available in specialty candy and gourmet food shops. If unavailable, substitute melted semisweet chocolate.*

1. Place 1½ cups hazelnuts in food processor; process until finely ground. (There should be ½ cup ground nuts; if necessary, process additional nuts.) Reserve remaining whole hazelnuts.

2. Beat butter, powdered sugar, lemon peel and salt in large bowl with electric mixer at medium speed until blended. Add egg; beat until blended. Gradually add ground hazelnuts and flour, beating until blended after each addition. Divide dough into quarters; shape each quarter into disc. Wrap and refrigerate 2 hours.

3. Preheat oven to 350°F. Line cookie sheets with parchment paper. Working with 1 disc at a time, roll out dough between parchment paper to ⅛- to ¹⁄₁₆-inch thickness. Cut out shapes with 1¼-inch round cookie cutter. Place ¾ inch apart on prepared cookie sheets.

4. Bake 8 minutes or until lightly browned. Cool completely on cookie sheets.

5. Spoon nougat paste into pastry bag fitted with ¼-inch round tip. Pipe about ¼ teaspoon paste onto centers of one third of cookies. Top with plain cookies; press gently. Spoon raspberry jam into pastry bag fitted with ⅓-inch round tip. Pipe about ⅓ teaspoon jam onto centers of second cookie layers. Top with plain cookies; press gently. Let stand 1 hour.

6. Melt chocolate and shortening in small heavy saucepan over low heat. Press cookie layers lightly together. Dip top of each cookie into chocolate mixture; shake to remove excess. Place cookies, chocolate side up, on wire racks; press 1 reserved whole hazelnut on top of each cookie. Let stand until chocolate is set.   *Makes about 4 dozen cookies*

Chocolate-Topped Linzer Cookies

Ginger Molasses Spice Cookies

2 cups all-purpose flour
1½ teaspoons ground ginger
1 teaspoon baking soda
½ teaspoon salt
½ teaspoon ground cinnamon
½ teaspoon ground cloves
1¼ cups sugar, divided
¾ cup (1½ sticks) butter, softened
¼ cup molasses
1 egg

1. Preheat oven to 375°F. Whisk flour, ginger, baking soda, salt, cinnamon and cloves in small bowl.

2. Beat 1 cup sugar and butter in large bowl with electric mixer at medium speed until light and fluffy. Add molasses and egg; beat until well blended. Gradually beat in flour mixture at low speed just until blended.

3. Place remaining ¼ cup sugar in shallow bowl. Shape dough by ½ teaspoonfuls into balls; roll in sugar to coat. Place 1 inch apart on ungreased cookie sheets.

4. Bake 8 minutes or until almost set. Cool on cookie sheets 2 minutes. Remove to wire racks; cool completely.

Makes about 12 dozen cookies

Ginger Molasses Spice Cookies

Mini Lemon Sandwich Cookies

     2 cups all-purpose flour
 1¼ cups (2½ sticks) butter, softened, divided
   ½ cup granulated sugar, divided
   ⅓ cup whipping cream
     1 teaspoon grated lemon peel
   ⅛ teaspoon lemon extract
   ¾ cup powdered sugar
     1 to 3 teaspoons lemon juice
     1 teaspoon vanilla
        Yellow food coloring (optional)

1. Beat flour, 1 cup butter, ¼ cup granulated sugar, cream, lemon peel and lemon extract in large bowl with electric mixer at medium speed until well blended. Divide dough into thirds; shape each third into disc. Wrap and refrigerate until firm.

2. Preheat oven to 375°F. Place remaining ¼ cup granulated sugar in shallow bowl.

3. Working with 1 disc at a time, roll out dough between parchment paper to ⅛-inch thickness. Cut out shapes with 1½-inch round cookie cutter. Dip both sides of cookies in sugar. Place 1 inch apart on ungreased cookie sheets; pierce several times with fork.

4. Bake 6 minutes or until slightly puffed but not browned. Cool on cookie sheets 1 minute. Remove to wire racks; cool completely.

5. Meanwhile, prepare filling. Beat powdered sugar, remaining ¼ cup butter, lemon juice and vanilla in medium bowl with electric mixer at low speed 2 minutes or until smooth. Tint with food coloring, if desired.

6. Spread ½ teaspoon filling on flat sides of half of cookies; top with remaining cookies.

Makes 4½ dozen sandwich cookies

Mini Lemon Sandwich Cookies

Mini Chocolate Whoopie Pies

1¾ cups all-purpose flour
½ cup unsweetened Dutch process cocoa powder
¾ teaspoon baking powder
½ teaspoon baking soda
½ teaspoon salt
1 cup packed brown sugar
1 cup (2 sticks) butter, softened, divided
1 egg
1½ teaspoons vanilla, divided
1 cup milk
1 cup marshmallow creme
1 cup powdered sugar

1. Preheat oven to 350°F. Line cookie sheets with parchment paper.

2. Sift flour, cocoa, baking powder, baking soda and salt into medium bowl. Beat brown sugar and ½ cup butter in large bowl with electric mixer at medium-high speed until light and fluffy. Beat in egg and 1 teaspoon vanilla until well blended. Alternately add flour mixture and milk, beating at low speed until smooth and well blended after each addition. Drop dough by heaping teaspoonfuls 2 inches apart onto prepared cookie sheets.

3. Bake 8 minutes or until puffed and tops spring back when lightly touched. Cool on cookie sheets 10 minutes. Remove to wire racks; cool completely.

4. Meanwhile, prepare filling. Beat remaining ½ cup butter, ½ teaspoon vanilla, marshmallow creme and powdered sugar in large bowl with electric mixer at high speed 2 minutes or until light and fluffy.

5. Spoon heaping teaspoon filling onto flat sides of half of cookies; top with remaining cookies. Store in airtight container in refrigerator. *Makes about 2 dozen sandwich cookies*

Mini Chocolate Whoopie Pies

Snowball Bites

1 package (about 16 ounces) refrigerated sugar cookie dough
¾ cup all-purpose flour
2 tablespoons honey or maple syrup
1 cup chopped walnuts or pecans
　Powdered sugar

1. Let dough stand at room temperature 15 minutes.

2. Beat dough, flour and honey in large bowl with electric mixer at medium speed until well blended. Stir in walnuts. Shape dough into disc. Wrap and refrigerate 2 hours or up to 2 days.

3. Preheat oven to 350°F. Shape dough into ¾-inch balls; place 1½ inches apart on ungreased cookie sheets.

4. Bake 10 minutes or until lightly browned. Roll warm cookies in powdered sugar. Remove to wire racks; cool completely. Just before serving, roll cookies in additional powdered sugar.

Makes about 2½ dozen cookies

Chocolate Chews

1 package (6 ounces) chow mein noodles
1 cup flaked coconut
1 cup semisweet chocolate chips
1 cup butterscotch-flavored chips
1 package (3 ounces) slivered almonds

1. Preheat oven to 350°F. Place noodles and coconut on cookie sheet in single layer. Bake 10 minutes or until crisp.

2. Melt chocolate and butterscotch chips in top of double boiler over simmering water. Remove from heat; stir in almonds, noodles and coconut. Drop mixture by teaspoonfuls onto waxed paper. Let stand until set.

Makes about 5 dozen chews

Snowball Bites

Chocolate Almond Sandwiches

1 package (about 16 ounces) refrigerated sugar cookie dough
4 ounces almond paste
¼ cup all-purpose flour
1 container (16 ounces) dark chocolate frosting
Sliced almonds

1. Let dough stand at room temperature 15 minutes.

2. Beat dough, almond paste and flour in large bowl with electric mixer at medium speed until well blended. Divide dough into thirds; freeze 20 minutes. Shape each third into 10×1-inch log. Wrap and refrigerate 2 hours or overnight. (Or freeze 1 hour or until firm.)

3. Preheat oven to 350°F. Lightly grease cookie sheets. Cut dough into ⅜-inch slices; place 2 inches apart on prepared cookie sheets.

4. Bake 10 minutes or until edges are lightly browned. Cool on cookie sheets 2 minutes. Remove to wire racks; cool completely.

5. Spread 2 teaspoons frosting on flat sides of half of cookies; top with remaining cookies. Spread small amount of frosting on top of each sandwich cookie; top with 1 sliced almond.

Makes about 2½ dozen sandwich cookies

Note: Almond paste is a prepared product made of ground blanched almonds, sugar and an ingredient such as glucose, glycerin or corn syrup to keep it pliable. It is often used as an ingredient in confections and baked goods. Almond paste is available in cans and plastic tubes in most supermarkets or gourmet food markets. After opening, wrap the container tightly and store it in the refrigerator.

Chocolate Almond Sandwiches

One-Bite Chocolate Chip Cookies

1¼ cups all-purpose flour
½ teaspoon baking soda
¼ teaspoon salt
½ cup (1 stick) butter, softened
½ cup packed light brown sugar
¼ cup granulated sugar
1 egg
1 teaspoon vanilla
1¼ cups mini semisweet chocolate chips
Sea salt (optional)

1. Preheat oven to 350°F. Whisk flour, baking soda and salt in small bowl.

2. Beat butter, brown sugar and granulated sugar in large bowl with electric mixer at medium speed until light and fluffy. Beat in egg and vanilla until well blended. Add flour mixture; beat at low speed until well blended. Stir in chocolate chips.

3. Drop dough by ½ teaspoonfuls 1 inch apart onto ungreased cookie sheets. Sprinkle very lightly with sea salt, if desired.

4. Bake 6 minutes or just until edges are golden brown. (Centers of cookies will be very light and will not look done.) Cool on cookie sheets 2 minutes. Remove to wire racks; cool completely.

Makes about 14 dozen cookies

One-Bite Chocolate Chip Cookies

Tiny Peanut Butter Sandwiches

1¼ cups all-purpose flour
½ teaspoon baking powder
½ teaspoon baking soda
¼ teaspoon salt
½ cup (1 stick) butter, softened
½ cup granulated sugar
½ cup packed brown sugar
½ cup creamy peanut butter
1 egg
1 teaspoon vanilla
1 cup semisweet chocolate chips
½ cup whipping cream

1. Preheat oven to 350°F. Whisk flour, baking powder, baking soda and salt in small bowl.

2. Beat butter, granulated sugar and brown sugar in large bowl with electric mixer at medium speed until light and fluffy. Beat in peanut butter, egg and vanilla until well blended. Gradually beat in flour mixture at low speed until blended.

3. Shape dough by ½ teaspoonfuls into balls; place 1 inch apart on ungreased cookie sheets. Flatten balls slightly in criss-cross pattern with tines of fork.

4. Bake 6 minutes or just until set. Cool on cookie sheets 4 minutes. Remove to wire racks; cool completely.

5. Meanwhile, prepare filling. Place chocolate chips in medium heatproof bowl. Place cream in small microwavable bowl; microwave on HIGH 2 minutes or just until simmering. Pour cream over chocolate chips. Let stand 2 minutes; stir until smooth. Let stand 10 minutes or until filling thickens to desired consistency.

6. Spread scant teaspoon filling on flat sides of half of cookies; top with remaining cookies.

Makes 6 to 7 dozen sandwich cookies

Tiny Peanut Butter Sandwiches

Pumpkin Whoopie Minis

1¾ cups all-purpose flour
2 teaspoons pumpkin pie spice
1 teaspoon baking powder
1 teaspoon baking soda
1 teaspoon salt, divided
1 cup packed brown sugar
½ cup (1 stick) butter, softened, divided
1 cup solid-pack pumpkin
2 eggs, beaten
¼ cup vegetable oil
1 teaspoon vanilla, divided
4 ounces cream cheese, softened
1½ cups powdered sugar

1. Preheat oven to 350°F. Line cookie sheets with parchment paper.

2. Combine flour, pumpkin pie spice, baking powder, baking soda and ¾ teaspoon salt in medium bowl. Beat brown sugar and ¼ cup butter in large bowl with electric mixer at medium speed until creamy. Beat in pumpkin, eggs, oil and ½ teaspoon vanilla until well blended. Beat in flour mixture at low speed just until blended. Drop dough by teaspoonfuls 2 inches apart onto prepared cookie sheets.

3. Bake 10 minutes or until springy to the touch. Cool on cookie sheets 5 minutes. Remove to wire racks; cool completely.

4. Meanwhile, prepare filling. Beat cream cheese and remaining ¼ cup butter in medium bowl with electric mixer until creamy. Beat in remaining ½ teaspoon vanilla and ¼ teaspoon salt until blended. Gradually add powdered sugar, beating until light and fluffy after each addition.

5. Spoon heaping teaspoon filling onto flat sides of half of cookies; top with remaining cookies. Store in airtight container in refrigerator.   *Makes about 2½ dozen sandwich cookies*

Pumpkin Whoopie Minis

Brownie Buttons

½ cup (1 stick) butter
2 squares (1 ounce each) unsweetened chocolate
1 cup sugar
2 eggs, at room temperature
½ cup all-purpose flour
¼ teaspoon salt
1 teaspoon vanilla
½ cup semisweet chocolate chips
¼ cup whipping cream
   Small chocolate nonpareil candies

1. Preheat oven to 325°F. Spray 8-inch square baking pan with nonstick cooking spray.

2. Melt butter and chocolate in small heavy saucepan over low heat. Remove from heat; gradually stir in sugar. Beat in eggs, one at a time, until blended. Stir in flour and salt. Stir in vanilla. Spread batter evenly in prepared pan.

3. Bake 25 minutes or until toothpick inserted into center comes out with fudgy crumbs. Cool completely in pan on wire rack; refrigerate until chilled before cutting.

4. Use 1¼-inch round cookie or biscuit cutter to cut out circles from brownies. Place brownies on wire rack set over waxed paper.

5. Place chocolate chips in small heatproof bowl. Place cream in small microwavable bowl; microwave on HIGH 1 minute or just until simmering. Pour cream over chocolate chips. Let stand 1 minute; stir until smooth. Let stand several minutes to thicken slightly; pour mixture over tops of brownies. Place candy in center of each brownie.

Makes about 2 dozen brownies

Brownie Buttons

Magic Minis

Banana Split Ice Cream Sandwiches

1 package (about 16 ounces) refrigerated chocolate chip cookie dough
2 bananas, mashed
½ cup strawberry jam, divided
4 cups strawberry ice cream, softened
Hot fudge topping
Whipped cream
9 maraschino cherries

1. Let dough stand at room temperature 15 minutes. Preheat oven to 350°F. Lightly grease 13×9-inch baking pan.

2. Beat dough and bananas in large bowl with electric mixer at medium speed until well blended. Spread dough evenly in prepared pan; smooth top. Bake 22 minutes or until edges are lightly browned. Cool completely in pan on wire rack.

3. Line 8-inch square baking pan with foil or plastic wrap, allowing some to hang over edges of pan. Remove cooled cookie from pan; cut in half crosswise. Place 1 cookie half, top side down, in 8-inch pan, trimming edges to fit, if necessary. Spread ¼ cup jam evenly over cookie. Spread ice cream evenly over jam. Spread remaining ¼ cup jam over bottom of remaining cookie half; place jam side down over ice cream. Wrap tightly with foil; freeze at least 2 hours or overnight.

4. Cut into bars and top with hot fudge topping, whipped cream and cherries.

Makes 9 servings

Petite Pudding Parfaits

2 ounces bittersweet or semisweet chocolate, chopped (or about ⅓ cup chips)

2 ounces white chocolate, chopped (or about ⅓ cup chips)

½ cup sugar

2 tablespoons flour

1 tablespoon cornstarch

⅛ teaspoon salt

2¼ cups milk

2 egg yolks, beaten

2 teaspoons vanilla

Chocolate curls or grated bittersweet chocolate (optional)

1. Place bittersweet chocolate and white chocolate in separate heatproof bowls; set aside.

2. Combine sugar, flour, cornstarch and salt in small saucepan. Gradually whisk in milk. Cook over medium heat until mixture comes to a boil, stirring constantly. Boil 2 minutes, stirring constantly.

3. Remove saucepan from heat. Stir small amount of hot mixture into egg yolks; return egg yolk mixture to saucepan. Cook and stir over low heat until thickened. Remove from heat; stir in vanilla.

4. Spoon half of egg yolk mixture over each chocolate; stir until melted.

5. For 2-ounce shot glasses, alternate layers of puddings using about 1 tablespoon pudding for each layer. Cover and refrigerate until chilled. Top with chocolate curls before serving, if desired.

Makes about 8 servings

Petite Pudding Parfaits

Rustic Apple Tartlets

    1 tablespoon butter
    4 medium Granny Smith, Crispin or other firm-fleshed apples, peeled and
        cut into ¾-inch chunks (about 4 cups)
    6 tablespoons granulated sugar
    ½ teaspoon ground cinnamon
    ⅛ teaspoon salt
    2 teaspoons cornstarch
    2 teaspoons lemon juice
    1 refrigerated pie crust (half of 15-ounce package)
    1 egg, beaten
    1 tablespoon coarse sugar

1. Melt butter in medium saucepan over medium heat; stir in apples, granulated sugar, cinnamon and salt. Cook 12 minutes or until apples are tender, stirring occasionally. Drain apples in colander set over medium bowl; pour liquid back into saucepan. Cook over medium-high heat until liquid is slightly syrupy and reduced by half. Stir in cornstarch; cook 1 minute.

2. Combine apples, lemon juice and cornstarch mixture in medium bowl; toss to coat. Let apple mixture cool to room temperature.

3. Preheat oven to 425°F. Line large rimmed baking sheet with parchment paper. Unroll dough onto clean work surface; cut out 5 circles with 4-inch round cookie cutter. Place dough circles on prepared baking sheet.

4. Divide apples evenly among dough circles, piling apples in center of each circle and leaving ½-inch border. Fold edge of dough up over filling, overlapping and pleating dough as necessary. Press dough gently to adhere to filling. Brush dough lightly with egg; sprinkle tartlets with coarse sugar.

5. Bake 25 minutes or until crusts are golden brown. Cool completely on wire rack.

Makes 5 tartlets

Rustic Apple Tartlets

Mini Strawberry Shortcakes

1 quart strawberries, hulled and sliced
½ cup sugar, divided
1 cup all-purpose flour
2 teaspoons baking powder
¼ teaspoon salt
¼ cup (½ stick) butter, cubed
1¼ cups whipping cream, divided

1. Combine strawberries and ¼ cup sugar in medium bowl; set aside.

2. Preheat oven to 425°F. Whisk flour, 2 tablespoons sugar, baking powder and salt in large bowl. Cut in butter with pastry blender or two knives until mixture resembles coarse crumbs. Gradually add ½ cup cream, stirring gently until dough comes together. (Dough will be slightly sticky.) Knead gently 4 to 6 times.

3. Pat dough into 6-inch square on lightly floured surface. Cut dough into 1½-inch squares with sharp knife. Place 1½ inches apart on ungreased baking sheet.

4. Bake 10 minutes or until golden brown. Remove to wire rack; cool slightly.

5. Meanwhile, beat remaining ¾ cup cream and 2 tablespoons sugar in small bowl with electric mixer at high speed until soft peaks form.

6. Split biscuits in half horizontally. Top bottom halves of biscuits with berry mixture, whipped cream and top halves of biscuits.

Makes 16 mini shortcakes

Mini Strawberry Shortcakes

Pumpkin Mousse Cups

  1¼ cups whipping cream, divided
    1 cup solid-pack pumpkin
  ⅓ cup sugar
  ½ teaspoon pumpkin pie spice
  ⅛ teaspoon salt
  ½ teaspoon vanilla
  ½ cup crushed gingersnap cookies (about 8 small gingersnaps)

1. Combine ½ cup cream, pumpkin, sugar, pumpkin pie spice and salt in small saucepan; bring to a simmer over medium heat. Reduce heat to low; simmer 15 minutes, stirring occasionally. Stir in vanilla; let cool to room temperature.

2. Beat remaining ¾ cup cream in small bowl with electric mixer at high speed until soft peaks form. Gently fold 1 cup whipped cream into pumpkin mixture until blended. Refrigerate until ready to serve. Spoon heaping ¼ cup pumpkin mousse into each of eight ½-cup glasses or dessert dishes. Top with dollop of remaining whipped cream; sprinkle with crushed cookies.

Makes 8 servings

Tiramisu Shots

  ¾ cup milk
  4 ounces cream cheese, softened
  1 package (about 1 ounce) dark chocolate hot cocoa mix
  1 cup coffee ice cream
  2 tablespoons cold strong coffee
  1 tablespoon amaretto liqueur (optional)
  1 teaspoon powdered sugar
12 miniature chocolate cordial cups (optional)
  Whipped cream and chocolate-covered espresso beans (optional)

Process milk, cream cheese and cocoa mix in blender until smooth. Add ice cream, coffee, amaretto, if desired, and powdered sugar; process until smooth. Pour into cordial cups, if desired, or shot glasses. Garnish with whipped cream and chocolate-covered espresso beans.

Makes 12 servings

Pumpkin Mousse Cups

Little Chocolate Chip Coffee Cakes

1⅓ cups all-purpose flour
¾ teaspoon baking powder
½ teaspoon salt
¼ teaspoon baking soda
¾ cup packed brown sugar
½ cup (1 stick) butter, softened
¼ cup granulated sugar
1 teaspoon vanilla
2 eggs
½ cup plus 3 tablespoons milk, divided
1½ cups semisweet chocolate chips, divided

1. Preheat oven to 350°F. Generously grease and flour 18 mini (¼-cup) bundt cups. Whisk flour, baking powder, salt and baking soda in small bowl.

2. Beat brown sugar, butter, granulated sugar and vanilla in large bowl with electric mixer at medium speed until light and fluffy. Beat in eggs, one at a time, until well blended. Alternately add flour mixture and ½ cup milk, beginning and ending with flour mixture, beating until blended after each addition. Stir in 1 cup chocolate chips. Spoon batter into prepared bundt cups, filling three-fourths full (about 3 tablespoons batter per cup).

3. Bake 16 minutes or until toothpick inserted into centers comes out clean. Cool in pan 5 minutes; invert onto wire racks to cool completely.

4. Combine remaining ½ cup chocolate chips and 3 tablespoons milk in small microwavable bowl. Microwave on HIGH 30 seconds; stir. Microwave at 15-second intervals until melted and smooth. Drizzle over cakes.

Makes 18 coffee cakes

Little Chocolate Chip Coffee Cakes

Jelly Doughnut Bites

½ cup plus 3 tablespoons warm (95 to 105°F) milk, divided
1¼ teaspoons active dry yeast
⅓ cup granulated sugar
1 tablespoon butter, softened
2½ cups all-purpose flour
1 egg
½ teaspoon salt
½ cup raspberry jam
Powdered sugar

1. Combine 3 tablespoons warm milk and yeast in large bowl. Let stand 5 minutes. Add granulated sugar, butter and remaining ½ cup milk; mix well. Add flour, egg and salt; beat with dough hook of electric mixer at medium speed until dough starts to climb up dough hook. If dough is too sticky, add additional flour, 1 tablespoon at a time.

2. Transfer dough to greased medium bowl; turn dough over to grease top. Cover and let stand in warm place 1 hour.

3. Grease 48 mini (1¾-inch) muffin cups. Punch down dough. Shape pieces of dough into 1-inch balls; place in prepared muffin cups. Cover and let stand 1 hour. Preheat oven to 375°F.

4. Bake 10 minutes or until golden brown. Remove to wire racks; cool completely.

5. Place jam in pastry bag fitted with small round tip. Insert tip into side of each doughnut; squeeze about 1 teaspoon jam into center. Sprinkle filled doughnuts with powdered sugar.

Makes 48 doughnut bites

Tip: These doughnuts are best eaten the same day they are made. They can be served warm or at room temperature. If desired, microwave on HIGH 10 seconds just before serving.

Jelly Doughnut Bites

Carrot Cake Minis

1 cup packed light brown sugar
¾ cup plus 2 tablespoons all-purpose flour
1 teaspoon baking soda
½ teaspoon salt
½ teaspoon ground cinnamon
¼ teaspoon ground nutmeg
⅛ teaspoon ground cloves
½ cup canola oil
2 eggs
1½ cups lightly packed grated carrots
½ teaspoon vanilla
Cream Cheese Frosting (recipe follows)
Toasted shredded coconut (optional)

1. Preheat oven to 350°F. Line 36 mini (1¾-inch) muffin cups with paper baking cups.

2. Whisk brown sugar, flour, baking soda, salt, cinnamon, nutmeg and cloves in large bowl. Stir in oil until blended. Add eggs, one at a time, stirring until blended after each addition. Stir in carrots and vanilla. Spoon batter evenly into prepared muffin cups.

3. Bake 15 minutes or until toothpick inserted into centers comes out clean. Cool in pans 5 minutes. Remove to wire racks; cool completely.

4. Meanwhile, prepare Cream Cheese Frosting. Frost cupcakes. Sprinkle with coconut, if desired. Cover and store in refrigerator.   *Makes 36 mini cupcakes*

Cream Cheese Frosting: Beat 1 package (8 ounces) softened cream cheese and ¼ cup (½ stick) softened butter in medium bowl with electric mixer at medium-high speed until creamy. Gradually beat in 1½ cups sifted powdered sugar until well blended. Beat in ¼ teaspoon salt and ¼ teaspoon vanilla. Makes about 3 cups.

Tip: Use a food processor to quickly grate the carrots for this recipe. Use the metal blade and pulse the carrots until they are evenly grated.

Carrot Cake Minis

Brownie Ice Cream Treats

½ cup all-purpose flour
½ teaspoon salt
¼ teaspoon baking powder
6 tablespoons butter
1 cup sugar
½ cup unsweetened Dutch process cocoa powder
2 eggs
½ teaspoon vanilla
2 cups pistachio or favorite flavor ice cream, slightly softened
Hot fudge topping, heated (optional)

1. Preheat oven to 350°F. Spray 9-inch square baking pan with nonstick cooking spray. Whisk flour, salt and baking powder in small bowl.

2. Melt butter in medium saucepan over low heat. Stir in sugar until blended. Stir in cocoa until well blended. Stir in eggs, one at a time, then vanilla. Stir in flour mixture until blended. Pour into prepared pan.

3. Bake 20 minutes or until toothpick inserted into center comes out with fudgy crumbs. Cool completely in pan on wire rack.

4. For 2¼-inch-wide jars, cut out 16 brownies using 2-inch round cookie or biscuit cutter. (See Tip.) Remove brownie scraps from pan (any pieces left between round cut-outs); crumble into small pieces. (Save remaining brownies for another use.)

5. Place 1 brownie in each of eight ½-cup glass jars. Top with 2 tablespoons ice cream, pressing to form flat layer over brownie. Repeat brownie and ice cream layers.

6. Drizzle with hot fudge topping, if desired. Sprinkle with brownie crumbs. Serve immediately. (Or make ahead, omitting hot fudge topping. Cover and freeze until ready to serve.)

Makes 8 servings

Tip: Measure the diameter of your jar first and cut out your brownies slightly smaller to fit in the jar. If your jars are too short to fit 2 brownie layers, cut the brownies in half horizontally with a serrated knife.

Brownie Ice Cream Treats

Chocolate Chip S'more Bites

1 package (about 16 ounces) refrigerated chocolate chip cookie dough
¾ cup semisweet chocolate chips
¼ cup plus 2 tablespoons whipping cream
½ cup marshmallow creme
½ cup sour cream

1. Preheat oven to 325°F. Spray 13×9-inch baking pan with nonstick cooking spray.

2. Press cookie dough into prepared pan, using damp hands to spread dough into even layer and cover bottom of pan. (Layer of dough will be very thin.) Bake 20 minutes or until light golden brown and just set. Cool completely in pan on wire rack.

3. Meanwhile, place chocolate chips in medium heatproof bowl. Place cream in small microwavable bowl; microwave on HIGH 1 minute or just until simmering. Pour cream over chocolate chips. Let stand 2 minutes; stir until smooth. Let stand 10 minutes or until thickened.

4. Combine marshmallow creme and sour cream in small bowl until smooth.

5. Cut bars into 1¼-inch squares with sharp knife. For each s'more, spread scant teaspoon chocolate mixture on bottom of one square; spread scant teaspoon marshmallow mixture on bottom of second square. Press together to form s'mores.   *Makes about 4 dozen s'mores*

Chocolate Chip S'more Bites

Dandy Candy

Malted Milk Balls

2½ cups small malted milk balls (½-inch diameter), coarsely crushed

1¾ cups chocolate graham cracker crumbs (9 to 11 crackers)

3 tablespoons unsweetened cocoa powder, divided

¼ teaspoon salt

1 cup mini marshmallows

½ cup light corn syrup

1 tablespoon honey

1 teaspoon rum extract

½ cup powdered sugar

1. Combine malted milk balls, graham cracker crumbs, 2 tablespoons cocoa and salt in large bowl. Chop marshmallows with remaining 1 tablespoon cocoa. Add to malted milk ball mixture; stir until blended.

2. Add corn syrup, honey and rum extract. Knead by hand until mixture comes together. Shape into 1-inch balls.

3. Spread powdered sugar on baking sheet; roll balls in sugar to coat.

Makes about 4 dozen balls

Tip: To make graham cracker crumbs, place crackers in food processor or blender and process until finely ground. Or place crackers in resealable food storage bag and use rolling pin to crush into fine crumbs. Malted milk balls can also be crushed in resealable food storage bag.

Variations: Substitute 1 teaspoon vanilla for the rum extract. Roll balls in unsweetened cocoa powder.

Mocha Fudge

1¾ cups sugar
¾ cup whipping cream
1 tablespoon instant coffee granules
1 tablespoon light corn syrup
1 cup milk chocolate chips
1 cup (half of 7-ounce jar) marshmallow creme
½ cup chopped nuts
1 teaspoon vanilla

1. Butter 8-inch square baking pan. Lightly butter side of medium heavy saucepan.

2. Combine sugar, cream, coffee granules and corn syrup in prepared saucepan. Cook over medium heat until sugar is dissolved and mixture comes to a boil, stirring constantly. Wash down side of saucepan with pastry brush frequently dipped in hot water to remove sugar crystals. Boil 5 minutes.

3. Meanwhile, combine chocolate chips, marshmallow creme, nuts and vanilla in medium heatproof bowl.

4. Pour sugar mixture over chocolate mixture; stir until chips are melted. Spread evenly in prepared pan. Score fudge into squares with knife. Refrigerate until firm.

5. Cut into squares. Store covered in refrigerator.

Makes about 1¾ pounds

Mocha Fudge

Double Peanut Fudge

1 cup powdered sugar
1 cup sweetened condensed milk
1 cup creamy peanut butter
2 tablespoons butter
½ teaspoon vanilla
1 cup chopped peanuts, divided

1. Line 8-inch square baking pan with parchment paper, extending 1 inch over edges of pan. Grease paper.

2. Combine powdered sugar, condensed milk, peanut butter, butter and vanilla in medium microwavable bowl. Microwave on HIGH 1 minute; stir. Microwave 1 minute; stir until smooth. Stir in ¾ cup peanuts. Spread evenly in prepared pan. Sprinkle with remaining ¼ cup peanuts. Refrigerate 2 hours or until firm.

3. Remove fudge with parchment paper from pan. Place on cutting board; remove and discard paper. Cut into ½-inch squares. Store covered in refrigerator.   *Makes about 1¼ pounds*

Pilgrim Hats

Yellow decorating icing
10 chocolate-covered cookies
10 mini peanut butter cups
Red and orange chewy fruit candies

1. Squeeze small amount of icing onto center of each cookie. Place peanut butter cup upside down on top of icing, pressing gently to adhere.

2. Pipe hatband and buckle around base of each peanut butter cup with icing.

3. Press candies with palm of hand to flatten. (Or stretch candies with fingers.) Cut out squares with scissors. Press 1 candy square into center of each buckle.   *Makes 10 hats*

Double Peanut Fudge

White Chocolate Triangles

        1 cup white chocolate chips
        ½ cup sweetened condensed milk
        ½ cup chopped pecans, toasted*
        ½ (9-ounce) package chocolate wafers, crushed

To toast pecans, spread in single layer on baking sheet. Bake in preheated 350°F oven 5 minutes or until golden brown, stirring frequently.

1. Grease 8-inch square baking pan. Combine chocolate chips and condensed milk in small heavy saucepan; cook and stir over low heat until melted and smooth. Stir in pecans and wafer crumbs.

2. Spread evenly in prepared pan; let stand until set. Cut into triangles. Store covered in refrigerator. Serve chilled or at room temperature.   *Makes 6 dozen triangles*

Little Christmas Puddings

        1 can (14 ounces) sweetened condensed milk
        1 square (1 ounce) semisweet chocolate
        2 teaspoons vanilla
     2¼ cups chocolate sandwich cookie crumbs
        ⅓ cup white chocolate chips
        Red and green holly decors

1. Combine condensed milk and semisweet chocolate in medium heavy saucepan; cook and stir over low heat until melted and smooth. Remove from heat; stir in vanilla.

2. Stir cookie crumbs into chocolate mixture until well blended. Cover and refrigerate 1 hour.

3. Line baking sheet with waxed paper. Shape heaping teaspoonfuls crumb mixture into 1-inch balls. Place on prepared baking sheet. Refrigerate until firm.

4. Place balls in 1¾-inch foil or paper baking cups. Place white chocolate chips in small microwavable bowl. Microwave on MEDIUM (50%) 2 minutes or until melted, stirring after each minute. Spoon melted white chocolate over tops. Decorate with decors. Let stand until set. Store covered in refrigerator.   *Makes about 3½ dozen treats*

White Chocolate Triangles

Maple-Pumpkin Fudge

2½ cups sugar
½ cup (1 stick) butter, cubed
1 can (5 ounces) evaporated milk
½ cup solid-pack pumpkin
1½ teaspoons pumpkin pie spice
1 package (12 ounces) white chocolate chips
1 jar (7 ounces) marshmallow creme
1 cup chopped walnuts
1½ teaspoons maple flavoring

1. Line 13×9-inch baking pan with foil, with ends of foil extending over edges of pan. Spray foil with nonstick cooking spray.

2. Combine sugar, butter, evaporated milk, pumpkin and pumpkin pie spice in large heavy saucepan. Bring to a boil over medium heat, stirring constantly. Reduce heat to medium-low; boil until candy thermometer reads 240°F, stirring constantly.

3. Stir in chocolate chips, marshmallow creme, nuts and maple flavoring. Remove from heat; stir constantly until chocolate is melted and satiny. Immediately pour into prepared pan (do not scrape side of saucepan) and spread evenly.

4. Let stand at room temperature until set. Refrigerate until firm. Use foil to lift fudge out of pan. Remove foil and cut into squares.

Makes 3 pounds

Maple-Pumpkin Fudge

Chocolate-Cherry Balls

1 cup chocolate graham cracker crumbs (6 to 7 crackers)
1 cup mini chocolate chips
¾ cup butter cookie crumbs (8 to 10 cookies)
⅛ teaspoon salt
½ cup prepared chocolate fudge frosting
¼ cup dark corn syrup
1 teaspoon vanilla
About 72 dried cherries
½ cup powdered sugar

1. Combine graham cracker crumbs, chocolate chips, cookie crumbs and salt in large bowl.

2. Add frosting, corn syrup and vanilla. Knead by hand until mixture comes together. Shape into 1-inch balls. Press 2 dried cherries into center of each ball and reshape mixture around cherries to cover.

3. Spread powdered sugar on baking sheet; roll balls in sugar to coat.

Makes about 3 dozen balls

Tip: To make graham cracker crumbs and cookie crumbs, place crackers and cookies in food processor or blender and process until finely ground. Or place crackers and cookies in resealable food storage bag and use rolling pin to crush into fine crumbs.

Variation: Roll balls in unsweetened cocoa powder.

Chocolate-Cherry Balls

Crème Brûlée Fudge

2½ cups granulated sugar
½ cup (1 stick) butter, cubed
1 can (5 ounces) evaporated milk
½ package (6 ounces) white chocolate chips
1 jar (7 ounces) marshmallow creme
1½ teaspoons vanilla
3 tablespoons turbinado sugar

1. Line 13×9-inch baking pan with foil, with ends of foil extending over edges of pan. Spray foil with nonstick cooking spray.

2. Combine granulated sugar, butter and evaporated milk in large heavy saucepan. Bring to a boil over medium heat, stirring constantly. Reduce heat to medium-low; boil until candy thermometer reads 240°F, stirring constantly.

3. Stir in chocolate chips, marshmallow creme and vanilla. Remove from heat; stir constantly until chocolate is melted and satiny. Immediately pour into prepared pan (do not scrape side of saucepan) and spread evenly.

4. Preheat broiler. Sprinkle top evenly with turbinado sugar. Broil 1 minute or until turbinado sugar is melted and browned (watch carefully). Let stand at room temperature until set. Refrigerate until firm. Use foil to lift fudge out of pan. Remove foil and cut into squares.

Makes 2½ pounds

Tip: Turbinado sugar is made by evaporating the juice from sugar cane. The result is coarse crystals with a golden color. It is natural and unrefined, and its flavor has a hint of molasses. Turbinado sugar is especially good sprinkled over cereal, fruit or baked goods, providing a subtle crunch.

Crème Brûlée Fudge

Coconut Bonbons

2 cups powdered sugar
1 cup flaked coconut
3 tablespoons evaporated milk
2 tablespoons butter, softened
1 teaspoon vanilla
1 cup semisweet chocolate chips
1 tablespoon shortening
   Toasted coconut (optional)
   Melted white chocolate (optional)

1. Line baking sheet with waxed paper.

2. Combine powdered sugar, coconut, evaporated milk, butter and vanilla in medium bowl. Shape into 1-inch balls; place on prepared baking sheet. Refrigerate until firm.

3. Combine chocolate chips and shortening in small microwavable bowl. Microwave on HIGH 1 minute; stir. Microwave at 30-second intervals, stirring after each interval, until melted and smooth.

4. Dip bonbons in chocolate mixture using toothpick or wooden skewer. Remove excess chocolate by scraping bottom of bonbon across bowl rim; return to prepared baking sheet. Sprinkle some bonbons with toasted coconut, if desired. Refrigerate all bonbons until firm. Drizzle plain bonbons with melted white chocolate, if desired. Store in airtight container in refrigerator.

Makes about 3 dozen bonbons

Gift Idea: Place the bonbons in petit fours or paper candy cups. Arrange some crinkled paper gift basket filler in the bottom of a tin or gift box and nestle the candies in the filler. Or, for party favors or small gifts, place three or four bonbons in a cellophane bag and tie it with two pieces of different colored curling ribbon.

Coconut Bonbons

Chunky Peanut Butter Fudge

1½ cups granulated sugar
1½ cups packed brown sugar
½ cup milk
1 tablespoon unsweetened cocoa powder
1 cup chunky peanut butter
½ cup (1 stick) butter, cubed
1 teaspoon vanilla

1. Grease 13×9-inch baking pan. Combine granulated sugar, brown sugar, milk and cocoa in large heavy saucepan. Cook over medium heat until candy thermometer reads 240°F, stirring constantly.

2. Remove from heat. Add peanut butter, butter and vanilla; stir until melted. Pour into prepared pan. Refrigerate until firm. Cut into 1-inch squares.   *Makes about 1¼ pounds*

Tropical Sugarplums

½ cup white chocolate chips
¼ cup light corn syrup
½ cup chopped dates
¼ cup chopped maraschino cherries, drained
1 teaspoon vanilla
¼ teaspoon rum extract
1¼ cups gingersnap cookie crumbs
Flaked coconut

1. Combine chocolate chips and corn syrup in medium heavy saucepan. Cook and stir over low heat until melted and smooth.

2. Stir in dates, cherries, vanilla and rum extract until well blended. Add gingersnap crumbs; stir until well blended. (Mixture will be stiff.)

3. Shape into ¾-inch balls; roll in coconut. Place in miniature paper candy cups, if desired. Serve immediately or let stand overnight to allow flavors to blend.

Makes about 2 dozen candies

Chunky Peanut Butter Fudge

Mississippi Mud Bars

¾ cup packed brown sugar
½ cup (1 stick) butter, softened
1 egg
1 teaspoon vanilla
½ teaspoon baking soda
¼ teaspoon salt
1 cup plus 2 tablespoons all-purpose flour
1 cup semisweet chocolate chips, divided
1 cup white chocolate chips, divided
½ cup chopped walnuts or pecans

1. Preheat oven to 375°F. Line 9-inch square baking pan with foil; grease foil.

2. Beat brown sugar and butter in large bowl with electric mixer at medium speed until well blended. Beat in egg and vanilla until blended. Beat in baking soda and salt. Add flour; beat at low speed until well blended. Stir in ⅔ cup semisweet chips, ⅔ cup white chips and walnuts. Spread evenly in prepared pan.

3. Bake 23 minutes or until center is set. Sprinkle with remaining ⅓ cup semisweet chips and ⅓ cup white chips. Let stand until chips soften; spread evenly over bars. Cool in pan on wire rack until chocolate is set. Cut into bars.   *Makes about 3 dozen bars*

METRIC CONVERSION CHART

VOLUME MEASUREMENTS (dry)

1/8 teaspoon = 0.5 mL
1/4 teaspoon = 1 mL
1/2 teaspoon = 2 mL
3/4 teaspoon = 4 mL
1 teaspoon = 5 mL
1 tablespoon = 15 mL
2 tablespoons = 30 mL
1/4 cup = 60 mL
1/3 cup = 75 mL
1/2 cup = 125 mL
2/3 cup = 150 mL
3/4 cup = 175 mL
1 cup = 250 mL
2 cups = 1 pint = 500 mL
3 cups = 750 mL
4 cups = 1 quart = 1 L

VOLUME MEASUREMENTS (fluid)

1 fluid ounce (2 tablespoons) = 30 mL
4 fluid ounces (1/2 cup) = 125 mL
8 fluid ounces (1 cup) = 250 mL
12 fluid ounces (1 1/2 cups) = 375 mL
16 fluid ounces (2 cups) = 500 mL

WEIGHTS (mass)

1/2 ounce = 15 g
1 ounce = 30 g
3 ounces = 90 g
4 ounces = 120 g
8 ounces = 225 g
10 ounces = 285 g
12 ounces = 360 g
16 ounces = 1 pound = 450 g

DIMENSIONS

1/16 inch = 2 mm
1/8 inch = 3 mm
1/4 inch = 6 mm
1/2 inch = 1.5 cm
3/4 inch = 2 cm
1 inch = 2.5 cm

OVEN TEMPERATURES

250°F = 120°C
275°F = 140°C
300°F = 150°C
325°F = 160°C
350°F = 180°C
375°F = 190°C
400°F = 200°C
425°F = 220°C
450°F = 230°C

BAKING PAN SIZES

Utensil	Size in Inches/Quarts	Metric Volume	Size in Centimeters
Baking or Cake Pan (square or rectangular)	8×8×2	2 L	20×20×5
	9×9×2	2.5 L	23×23×5
	12×8×2	3 L	30×20×5
	13×9×2	3.5 L	33×23×5
Loaf Pan	8×4×3	1.5 L	20×10×7
	9×5×3	2 L	23×13×7
Round Layer Cake Pan	8×1½	1.2 L	20×4
	9×1½	1.5 L	23×4
Pie Plate	8×1¼	750 mL	20×3
	9×1¼	1 L	23×3
Baking Dish or Casserole	1 quart	1 L	—
	1½ quart	1.5 L	—
	2 quart	2 L	—